Collins

Science

KS3

Revision Guide

KS3 Revision
Science

**Byron Dawson and
Eliot Attridge**

Contents

Cells – the Building Blocks of Life

You must be able to:

- Use a microscope to help understand the functions of the cell
- Remember the differences between animal and plant cells
- Understand how substances move into and out of cells by diffusion
- Understand the organisation of cells.

Using a Light Microscope

- Cells are too small to see with the naked eye. Using a light microscope helps us to see and draw cells.

A plant cell drawn after observation with a light microscope

cell wall →
nucleus ←
chloroplast ←
vacuole →
cell membrane →
cytoplasm ←
mitochondria ←

> **Key Point**
>
> Objects need to be placed on a slide, stained and covered with a coverslip, placed on the 'stage' of the microscope, illuminated and then focussed.

How Plant and Animal Cells Work

- Animal and plant cells share some features but not others.
- Different parts of animal and plant cells have different functions.

Part	Function	Animal Cells?	Plant Cells?
Membrane	Controls what enters and leaves the cell	Yes	Yes
Cytoplasm	Place where lots of chemical reactions (photosynthesis) take place	Yes	Yes
Nucleus	Stores information (in DNA) and controls what happens in the cell	Yes	Yes
Mitochondria	Release energy from food (glucose) by aerobic respiration	Yes	Yes
Cell wall	Made from cellulose and gives rigid support to the cell	No	Yes
Vacuole	Inflates the cell like air pumped into a tyre and provides support to the cell	No	Usually
Chloroplast	Contains green chlorophyll that changes sunlight energy into glucose food energy	No	Yes

Diffusion

- **Diffusion** is one of the ways that substances enter and leave cells.
- In an animal cell, oxygen and glucose diffuse through the membrane into the cell. This is because there is more oxygen and glucose outside the cell than there is inside.
- Carbon dioxide and waste products diffuse out of the cell into the blood.
- In a plant cell, carbon dioxide diffuses in. Oxygen and glucose diffuse out.

Unicellular Organisms

- **Unicellular** organisms have just one cell.
- *Euglena* has a long whip-like structure to help it move through water.
- *Amoeba* can make finger-like projections to catch food.

Organisation of Cells

- Cells of the same type carrying out the same function are usually grouped together to form a **tissue**, e.g. skin cells.
- Different types of tissue are grouped together to form **organs**, e.g. the brain.
- Different types of organs are grouped together to form **organ systems**, e.g. the nervous system.
- Different types of organ systems work together to form the organism, e.g. a human being.
- Examples of cell and organ systems include:
  - Bone cells in the skeletal system
  - Blood cells in the transport system
  - Nerve cells in the nervous system
  - Sperm cells in the reproductive system.

 Key Point

Diffusing substances always move from where there is a lot of the substance (high concentration) to where there is very little (low concentration).

Amoeba as seen through a microscope

 Key Point

cells ➡ tissues ➡ organs ➡ systems ➡ organisms

Key Words

membrane
cytoplasm
nucleus
mitochondria
cell wall
vacuole
chloroplast
diffusion
unicellular
tissue
organ
organ system

Quick Test

1. Name one structure that is found in plant cells but not animal cells.
2. Where in a cell is energy released from food?
3. Name the process where molecules move from where there are lots of them to where there are only a few.
4. Put these words in order of complexity starting with 'cell': cell, organism, organ, system, tissue.

Cells – the Building Blocks of Life

You must be able to:

- Understand and explain the structure of the human reproductive system and how it works
- Know how reproduction and fruit dispersal works in a flowering plant
- Understand why plant reproduction is important to humans.

Reproduction in Humans

- Sexual reproduction in humans involves males and females. Males produce sperm cells in the testes. Females produce egg cells in the ovary.
- The penis deposits the sperm in the female vagina.
- Sperm swim up through the uterus to the oviduct.
- Fertilisation occurs when a sperm cell joins with an egg cell.
- The fertilised egg then grows into an embryo and eventually becomes a baby.

Fertilisation in animals

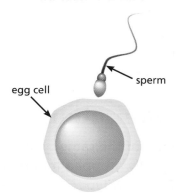

sperm

egg cell

Female reproductive system

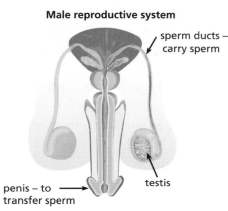

uterus

oviduct – carries egg to uterus

cervix

egg

ovary

vagina – through which baby is born

Male reproductive system

sperm ducts – carry sperm

penis – to transfer sperm

testis

Menstrual Cycle

- Females have a menstrual cycle lasting for about 28 days. This is called menstruation.
- On days 1–5, if pregnancy has not occurred, the uterus lining breaks down, tissue and blood are lost, and is replaced with new tissue.
- Fertilisation can only occur on or around day 14 when an egg is released from the ovary.

Gestation

- Gestation is the process of the embryo developing in the womb.
- The growing baby receives food and oxygen from the mother's blood through the placenta and umbilical cord.
- Therefore, if the mother smokes and drinks alcohol the baby will also receive some of the alcohol and nicotine.
- In humans, gestation ends after nine months with the birth of the baby.

> **Key Point**
>
> A human foetus takes 38 weeks to grow from the cell being fertilised to a baby.

Reproduction in Flowering Plants

- Some flowers are insect pollinated, e.g. a rose.
  - Insects visit flowers to collect sweet **nectar**
  - They transfer pollen from the **anther** of one flower to the **stigma** of another flower
  - The male pollen fertilises the female egg cell.
- Some flowers are wind pollinated, e.g. grass.
  - Wind blows pollen from one flower to another
  - Wind pollinated flowers do not have a scent or nectar and petals are not brightly coloured as they do not need to attract insects
  - They have a feathery stigma to catch the pollen.

> ### Key Point
>
> **Pollination** is the transfer of pollen by insect or wind from the anther of one flower to the stigma of another.
>
> Fertilisation is when male and female sex cells join.

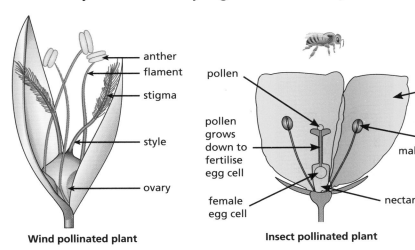

Wind pollinated plant

anther
flament
stigma
style
ovary

pollen
pollen grows down to fertilise egg cell
female egg cell
petal
anther makes pollen
nectar

Insect pollinated plant

Dispersal

- After fertilisation, seeds develop inside fruits. These then must be spread over a large area by **dispersal**.
- Some fruit and seeds are spread by animals, e.g. some seeds have hooks which stick to an animal's fur.
- Some are spread by wind. These often have wings or parachutes to be carried by the breeze, e.g. sycamore and dandelion seeds.
- Plants produce many seeds as most fail to grow into a new plant.

The Importance of Plant Reproduction

- Plants provide us with most of our food.
- Without insects to pollinate the flowers, many of us would starve due to lack of food.

> ### Key Words
>
> sperm
> testes
> egg cell
> ovary
> uterus
> fertilisation
> embryo
> menstruation
> gestation
> nectar
> anther
> stigma
> pollination
> dispersal

> ### Quick Test
>
> 1. Which two cells join together at fertilisation?
> 2. On which day of the menstrual cycle is a female egg released?
> 3. Write down the differences between an insect pollinated flower and a wind pollinated flower.
> 4. List two ways that fruits and seeds can be dispersed.

Eating, Drinking and Breathing

You must be able to:

- Know and explain how humans move air into and out of lungs
- Know and understand how oxygen and carbon dioxide move between the blood and the lungs
- Understand the effect of exercise, asthma and smoking on the breathing systems.

Breathing

- Breathing involves moving air into and out of the lungs.

When breathing in:

1. Ribs move up and out
2. **Diaphragm** flattens and moves down
3. Space inside the lungs increases
4. This increases the volume and reduces the pressure
5. Air rushes into the lungs from outside.

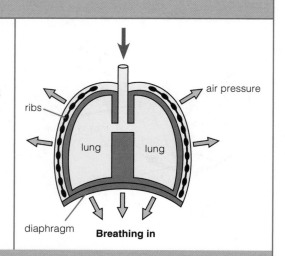

ribs · air pressure · lung · lung · diaphragm

Breathing in

When breathing out:

1. Ribs move down and in
2. Diaphragm moves up
3. Space inside the lungs decreases
4. This decreases the volume and increases the pressure
5. Air is pushed out of the lungs.

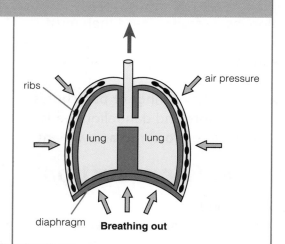

ribs · air pressure · lung · lung · diaphragm

Breathing out

> **Key Point**
>
> When we breathe in, air is pushed in by **air pressure** from the outside.

Gas Exchange

- The lungs are made of millions of tiny air sacs called alveoli.
- These air sacs are:
  - Thin
  - Moist
  - Have a good blood supply
  - Have a large surface area.

Structure of alveoli

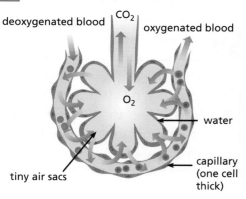

deoxygenated blood · CO_2 · oxygenated blood · O_2 · water · tiny air sacs · capillary (one cell thick)

- Gas exchange is when:
  - Carbon dioxide leaves the blood and enters the lungs to be breathed out
  - Oxygen leaves the lungs and enters the blood.
- Gas exchange happens through the thin walls of the air sacs.
- The exchange happens because of diffusion (see page 4).

The breathing system

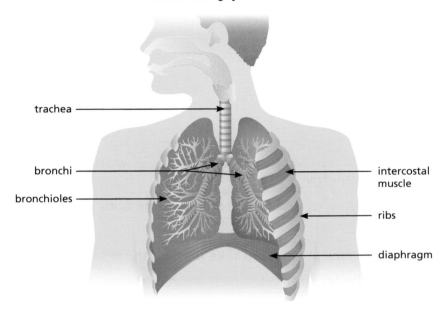

trachea

bronchi

bronchioles

intercostal muscle

ribs

diaphragm

> **Key Point**
>
> Diffusion is the movement of particles from a high to a low concentration.

Things that Affect our Breathing

Things that Affect Breathing	Effect on Breathing
Exercise	<ul><li>Increases lung size.</li><li>Improves gas exchange.</li></ul>
Asthma	<ul><li>Causes breathing tubes (bronchioles) to narrow, making breathing difficult.</li></ul>
Smoking	<ul><li>Damages the breathing tubes so that mucus builds up. This causes a cough, makes breathing more difficult and makes infections more likely.</li><li>In the long term can cause emphysema and lung cancer.</li></ul>

> **Quick Test**
>
> 1. Explain how the ribs and diaphragm move to make you breathe in.
> 2. Explain what happens to the volume and pressure inside the lungs when the ribs move down and in.
> 3. Name the process by which oxygen moves from the air in our lungs into the blood.
> 4. Describe the effect smoking has on the lungs.

> **Key Words**
>
> diaphragm
> air pressure
> alveoli
> asthma

Eating, Drinking and Breathing

You must be able to:

- Explain what is meant by a healthy diet
- Explain the energy content of a healthy diet and understand what happens when a healthy diet becomes unbalanced
- Know and explain the jobs of different parts of the digestive system.

A Healthy Diet

- A healthy diet contains all the right proportions of the following substances:

Content of Healthy Diet	Purpose
Carbohydrate	Gives the body energy
Fat	Gives the body energy and can be stored in the body
Protein	Used for growth
Vitamins	Used to help chemical reactions take place in the body
Minerals	Used to make bones strong and help the blood carry oxygen
Fibre	Helps undigested food pass quickly through the gut
Water	Dissolves chemicals so that chemical reactions can take place

- A healthy diet also contains sufficient food to provide us with just the right amount of energy.
- Energy in food is measured in calories or joules.
- 1 calorie = 4.2 joules
- A young man needs about 2500 kcal per day.
- 2500 kcal × 4.2 joules = 10,500 kJ per day.

> **Key Point**
>
> When dieticians talk about calories in food they really mean kilocalories. A kilocalorie is 1000 calories.

An Unbalanced Diet

- Eating an unbalanced diet can cause many problems:

Cause	Problem
Eating too much	Obesity
Eating too little	Starvation/malnutrition
Not eating enough protein	Kwashiorkor, an illness caused by severe protein deficiency. It is mostly seen in developing countries.
Not eating enough vitamins	A lack (or deficiency) of different vitamins causes different diseases, e.g. a lack of vitamin C causes scurvy.
Not eating enough minerals	A lack of iron causes anaemia. A lack of calcium causes soft bones.

The Digestive System

- The digestive system processes food that is eaten in the mouth. Food travels through the oesophagus, stomach, intestine and rectum until the waste is eliminated from the anus.
- The pancreas also plays a key role in digestion by producing digestive enzymes which help break down the food.

The digestive system

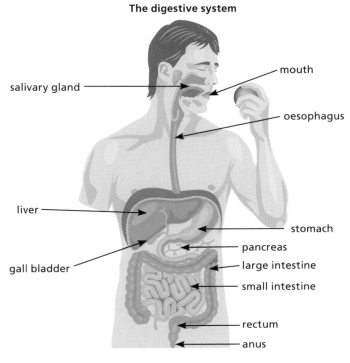

- salivary gland
- mouth
- oesophagus
- liver
- stomach
- pancreas
- large intestine
- gall bladder
- small intestine
- rectum
- anus

Food in Plants

- Unlike animals that eat food, plants make their own food.
- The process is called photosynthesis.
- Plants take water and minerals from the soil.
- They take carbon dioxide from the air.
- They use energy from the Sun to convert these substances into carbohydrates in their leaves:

light
water + carbon dioxide ➜ **glucose + oxygen**
chlorophyll

> **Key Point**
>
> Animals eat food, plants make it.

> **Key Words**
>
> carbohydrate
> fat
> protein
> vitamins
> minerals
> fibre
> kwashiorkor
> scurvy
> anaemia
> oesophagus
> stomach
> intestine
> rectum
> anus
> pancreas
> photosynthesis

> **Quick Test**
>
> 1. Name five components of a healthy diet.
> 2. Name three possible consequences of eating an unbalanced diet.
> 3. Write down the different parts of the digestive system in the order food travels through them. Start with **mouth**.
> 4. Describe the difference in feeding between plants and animals.

Key Stage 2 Concepts

1 All living organisms have certain things in common.

a) Copy the table below and put a tick (✔) in the box next to the characteristics found in all living things.

Hardness	
Nutrition	
Transparent	
Flying	
Flexible	
Growth	
Reproduction	
Melting	

[3]

b) One of the characteristics of living things is movement. Human beings use a skeleton to help them move. The skeleton also protects different parts of the body.

Trace or sketch the diagram of the skeleton.

i) Draw a **J** on the diagram to show the position of a joint for movement. [1]

ii) Draw a **P** on the diagram to show part of the skeleton that protects the body. [1]

2 Materials have many different properties. Jack found these materials in his father's shed.

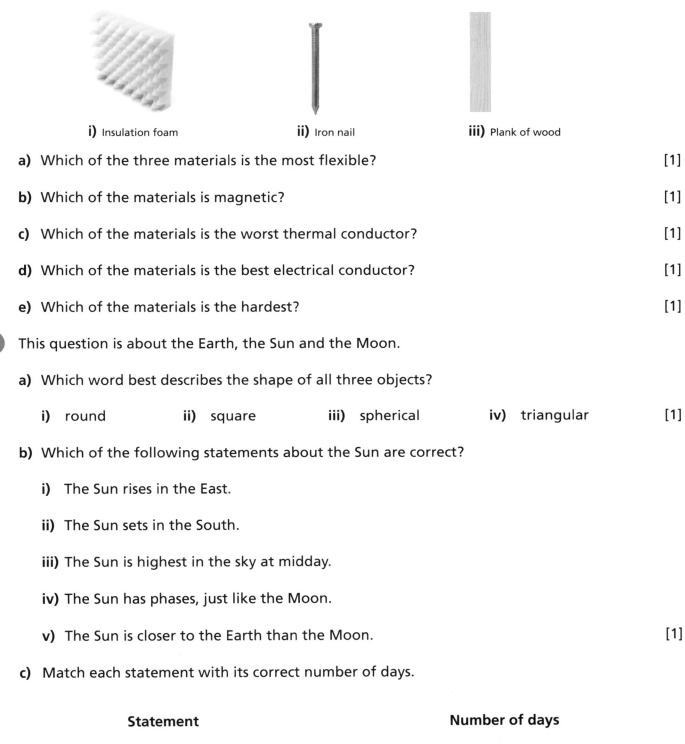

i) Insulation foam ii) Iron nail iii) Plank of wood

a) Which of the three materials is the most flexible? [1]

b) Which of the materials is magnetic? [1]

c) Which of the materials is the worst thermal conductor? [1]

d) Which of the materials is the best electrical conductor? [1]

e) Which of the materials is the hardest? [1]

3 This question is about the Earth, the Sun and the Moon.

a) Which word best describes the shape of all three objects?

   i) round   ii) square   iii) spherical   iv) triangular   [1]

b) Which of the following statements about the Sun are correct?

   i) The Sun rises in the East.

   ii) The Sun sets in the South.

   iii) The Sun is highest in the sky at midday.

   iv) The Sun has phases, just like the Moon.

   v) The Sun is closer to the Earth than the Moon.   [1]

c) Match each statement with its correct number of days.

Statement		Number of days
The Earth orbits the Sun		28
The Earth rotates once		1
The Moon orbits the Earth		365

[3]

Cells – the Building Blocks of Life

1   Match the part of a cell to its function.

Part of cell	Function
Membrane	Changes light energy into food energy
Cytoplasm	Inflates the cell
Nucleus	Supports the cell
Mitochondria	Releases energy from glucose
Cell wall	Stores information and controls the cell
Vacuole	Where chemical reactions take place
Chloroplast	Controls what enters and leaves a cell

[7]

2   These plant cells were seen using a microscope. Make a labelled drawing of one of them.

[6]

3   Which of these words describes how substances can enter or leave a cell?

 i) cytoplasm   **ii)** vacuole   **iii)** diffusion   [1]

Eating, Drinking and Breathing

1 Humans need to eat a healthy diet.

    a) Explain what is meant by a healthy diet. [2]

    b) Write down three things that can happen if we do not have a healthy diet.

        Explain your three answers. [3]

2 Look at the diagram of the digestive system.

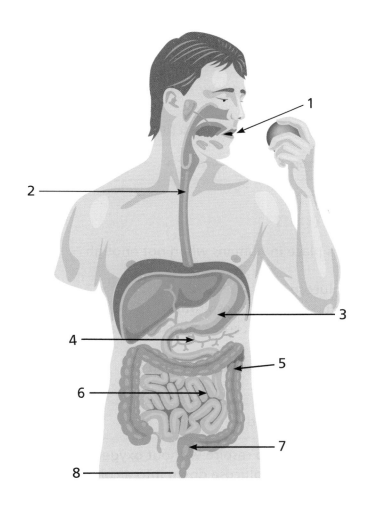

    a) Give the correct names for each part 1–8. [8]

    b) Explain what each of the parts you have labelled does. [8]

3 Explain the difference between feeding in animals and feeding in plants. [4]

Getting the Energy your Body Needs

You must be able to:

- Explain what respiration is
- Understand and explain aerobic and anaerobic respiration, including the differences between them.

Respiration

- **Respiration** is the process by which organisms release energy from food.
- The energy is needed to power all the chemical processes necessary for life.
- There are two types of respiration, aerobic and anaerobic.

Aerobic Respiration

- Humans release energy from glucose and oxygen by aerobic respiration.
- Carbon dioxide and water are produced as waste products.

glucose + oxygen ⟶ carbon dioxide + water + energy

Anaerobic Respiration

- Anaerobic respiration takes place in humans when not enough oxygen is available.
- Humans can break down glucose into lactic acid.
- Less energy is released during anaerobic respiration.
- Lactic acid is also released. This quickly causes muscle pain and fatigue.
- 'Getting the burn' is when muscles produce lactic acid in anaerobic respiration.

glucose ⟶ lactic acid + energy

- Yeast is a microorganism that can also respire without oxygen (anaerobic respiration). Yeast breaks glucose down into alcohol and carbon dioxide.
- This process is called fermentation.

glucose ⟶ alcohol + carbon dioxide + energy

> **Key Point**
>
> Although humans can respire without oxygen we can only do this for a very short time. It happens when we need a lot of oxygen very quickly, such as when we run a fast race.

> **Key Point**
>
> Fermentation is used to produce alcoholic drinks such as wine and beer.

Similarities and Differences between Aerobic and Anaerobic Respiration

	Aerobic	Anaerobic
Use glucose	✔	✔
Use oxygen	✔	✗
Produce carbon dioxide	✔	✔ Fermentation in yeast ✗ but not in humans
Produce water	✔	✗
Release *lots* of energy	✔	✗
Can produce lactic acid	✗	✔ In humans ✗ but not by fermentation
Can produce alcohol	✗	✔ Fermentation in yeast ✗ but not in humans
Causes muscle fatigue	✗	✔

Quick Test

1. What is the type of respiration that uses oxygen?
2. Name the type of respiration that releases the most energy.
3. Give the type of respiration that can produce lactic acid.
4. Which type of respiration occurs during fermentation?
5. Other than carbon dioxide, what substance is produced during fermentation?

Key Words

respiration
aerobic
anaerobic
glucose
oxygen
lactic acid
fermentation

Getting the Energy your Body Needs

You must be able to:

- Explain the structure and function of the human skeleton
- Explain how muscles make the skeleton move.

The Human Skeleton

- The human skeleton has several different functions:
  - Supports the body and gives it shape.
  - Acts as a framework that enables muscles to move the body.
  - Protects parts of the body, for example, the skull protects the brain and the ribs protect the heart and lungs.
  - Makes red blood cells in the marrow of the long bones, for example, humerus and femur.

Bone marrow

Human skeleton

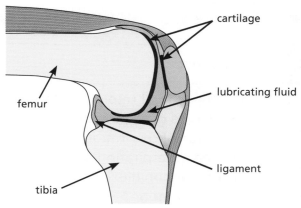

skull

ribs

humerus

spine

elbow joint

ulna and radius

hip joint

femur

kneecap

Joints and Muscles

- Bones in the skeleton are held together in **joints**.
- Joints allow the skeleton to move.
- Joints are held together by **ligaments**.
- The end of each bone is covered in **cartilage** for a smooth surface that cushions the joint.
- The joint is filled with a fluid that lubricates the joint.

The knee

cartilage

lubricating fluid

femur

ligament

tibia

Muscles and Force

- Muscles move joints.
- Muscles are attached to bones by tendons.
- Each joint needs two muscles to make it work. This is called an antagonistic pair.
- One muscle moves the joint in one direction. The other muscle moves the joint in the opposite direction.
- Muscles work by contracting and getting shorter in length. This pulls the bone and moves the joint.

> **Key Point**
>
> Some muscles work in pairs called antagonistic pairs. When one muscle contracts the other muscle relaxes.

Muscles in the arm

- The force exerted by muscles can be measured in Newtons.
- To work out the force applied by a muscle multiply the mass lifted by its distance from the joint.
- The answer is mass × distance from joint equals force × distance from the same joint. So in the diagram:

10 kg × 30 cm = 300   ? N × 5 cm = 300   therefore the force (?) = 60 N

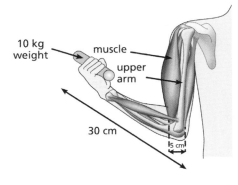

> **Quick Test**
>
> 1. Give four functions performed by the skeleton.
> 2. Name the tissue that attaches bones to each other in a joint.
> 3. Name the tissue that attaches muscle to bone.
> 4. Explain what antagonistic means.

> **Key Words**
>
> joint
> ligament
> cartilage
> tendon
> antagonistic pair

Looking at Plants and Ecosystems

You must be able to:

- Explain how photosynthesis takes place
- Understand how a green leaf is adapted for photosynthesis
- Understand the importance of photosynthesis to other living things.

Photosynthesis

- **Photosynthesis** is the process by which green plants make food.
- Green plants absorb energy from sunlight.
- They use the energy to react water with carbon dioxide to make **glucose**.
- The energy is stored in the glucose.
- **Oxygen** is released as a waste product.
- Plants use a green chemical called **chlorophyll** inside **chloroplasts** to perform photosynthesis.

> **light**
> **water + carbon dioxide** ➞ **glucose + oxygen**
> **chlorophyll**

> ### Key Point
>
> When you write down the word equation for photosynthesis always include light and chlorophyll.

Leaves and Photosynthesis

- Leaves are the plant's factory where photosynthesis takes place.
- Leaves are adapted to do this job because they:
    - Are thin – this stops the leaves from being heavy, enabling trees to have more leaves and therefore a larger surface area
    - Have a large surface area – to catch as much sunlight as possible
    - Are green, because of the chemical chlorophyll they use in order to photosynthesise
    - Have small holes called **stomata** on the underside of the leaf to let in carbon dioxide and let out oxygen. A single hole is called a **stoma**
    - Have tiny tubes called xylem to carry water and minerals up from the roots
    - Have tiny tubes called phloem to carry glucose away for storage.

Inside of a leaf

upper layer

chloroplasts

lower layer

stoma

The Importance of Photosynthesis

- Plants and animals depend on each other for survival – they are interdependent.
- Plants provide animals with food (glucose) and oxygen.
- Animals provide plants with carbon dioxide that they need for photosynthesis.
- Photosynthesis builds up complex glucose molecules from simple molecules (water and carbon dioxide). This stores energy.
- Respiration breaks down complex glucose molecules into simple molecules and releases energy.

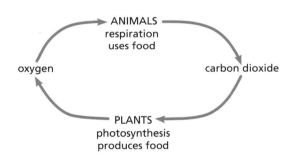

ANIMALS
respiration
uses food

oxygen

carbon dioxide

PLANTS
photosynthesis
produces food

- Most animals on Earth depend on plants for glucose, and oxygen to breathe.
- Most glucose and oxygen are produced by plants in the rain forest and algae in the oceans.

> **Key Point**
>
> Photosynthesis and respiration are the opposite of each other.
>
> - Respiration uses food and oxygen, and produces carbon dioxide.
> - Photosynthesis uses carbon dioxide, and produces food and oxygen.

> **Key Words**
>
> photosynthesis
> glucose
> oxygen
> chlorophyll
> chloroplast
> stomata
> stoma
> interdependent

Quick Test

1. Write down the word equation for photosynthesis.
2. State how photosynthesis is different to respiration.
3. Write down three different parts of a leaf and say how each one helps photosynthesis to take place.
4. Explain how plants and animals depend upon one another.
5. Explain what interdependence means.

Looking at Plants and Ecosystems

You must be able to:

- Use food webs to explain relationships between different organisms
- Understand how organisms are affected by the environment
- Understand how differences between organisms help them to survive.

Humans and Their Food Supply

- A good food supply is important for humans.
- This food supply depends on how organisms transfer energy from one to another.
- This means that organisms in an environment are interdependent in many ways.
- Insects **pollinate** flowers so seeds and fruit can grow and be used as food by other animals.
- Humans rely on insect pollinators for many of our crops.
- Insecticides can kill harmful insects and pests, but can also kill useful pollinators.

Interdependence of Organisms

- The best way to show how organisms depend on one another is to draw a **food web**.
- Food webs are made up from many different **food chains**. They are all interdependent.
- A food chain describes what eats what in a community.
- Interdependence describes how all the living organisms in an **environment** depend upon one another.
- Food webs show how organisms depend upon one another for food; they show relationships between organisms.
- **Producers** are plants. They produce food by photosynthesis.
- **Consumers** are animals. They consume food for energy.

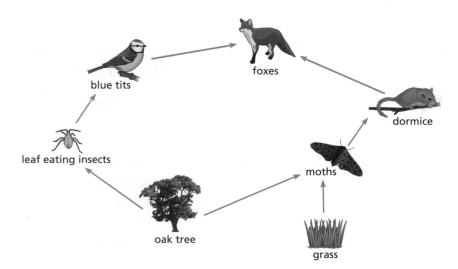

Organisms and the Environment

- Sometimes poisonous waste can get into an ecosystem:
  1 Plants at the bottom of the food web absorb the poison.
  2 The poison is passed on to the animals that feed upon them.
  3 Because these animals eat lots of plants they absorb more of the poison.
  4 The poison accumulates as it is passed up the food web; this is called bioaccumulation.
  5 Eventually there is enough poison in the animals at the top of the food web to kill them:

Poison in a food web

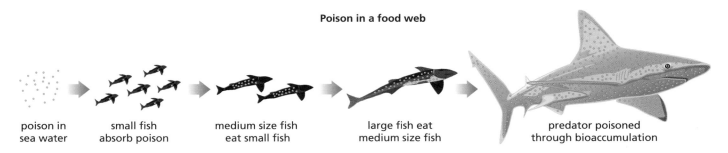

| poison in sea water | small fish absorb poison | medium size fish eat small fish | large fish eat medium size fish | predator poisoned through bioaccumulation |

- Bioaccumulation occurs because there are many more organisms at the bottom of a food chain and only a few predators at the top.
- This forms a pyramid of numbers that means poisons accumulate in greater numbers in the top predators.

Variation Between Organisms

- Most living organisms are different from one another. This is called variation.
- Different species have different characteristics.
- Different species survive in the same ecosystem because they are adapted to survive in different parts of the ecosystem.
- For example, different parts of the ecosystem are called niches.
- Fish live in water so they have gills; birds fly, so they have wings.
- Variation means that certain members of a species are more likely to survive when the environment changes.

> **Key Words**
>
> pollinate
> food web
> food chain
> environment
> producers
> consumers
> bioaccumulation
> pyramid of numbers
> variation
> species
> niches

> **Quick Test**
>
> 1. What do arrows on a food web show?
> 2. What does bioaccumulation mean?
> 3. Explain why variation between different organisms is important.

Cells – the Building Blocks of Life

1 Unicellular organisms have different structures from each other.

Explain why. [2]

2 Match the type of cell with the correct organ system.

Type of Cell	Organ system
Bone cell	Transport system
Red blood cell	Skeletal system
Nerve cell	Reproductive system
Sperm cell	Nervous system

[4]

3 Copy and complete this table by putting a ✔ and a ✗ next to each part of the reproductive system.

Part	Male	Female
Testis		
Egg cell		
Vagina		
Sperm		
Penis		

[5]

4 Write down the differences between insect and wind pollinated flowers. [3]

5 Insects are important for our food supply.

Explain why. [2]

6 Pollination requires the transfer of pollen from one flower to another.
This means the grains have to be very small.

Describe how you would use a light microscope to look at pollen grains. [6]

Eating, Drinking and Breathing

1 Look at the diagram. It shows how we breathe in and out. Use the diagram to explain what is happening when we:
- breathe in   [3]
- breathe out   [3]

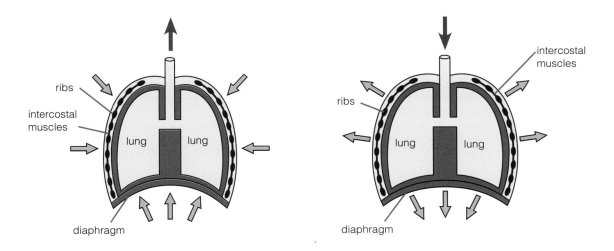

2 Write down three different things that can affect the human breathing system.   [3]

3 Write down why a balanced diet should contain each of the following things:
carbohydrate, fat, protein, vitamins, minerals, fibre, water   [7]

4 Explain the importance of bacteria in the digestive system.   [2]

5 An enzyme is a biological catalyst. Explain what this means.   [2]

6 The following statements describe the roles of some organs associated with the
digestive system.
One of the statements is incorrect.
Copy the table and put a cross (✗) against the incorrect statement.

The oesophagus joins the mouth to the stomach	
The stomach produces an acid to break down food	
The small intestine is where water is absorbed	
Waste material leaves the body through the anus	

[1]

Getting the Energy your Body Needs

1 Copy and complete the table by putting a tick (✔) in the correct box next to each statement about respiration.

	Aerobic	Anaerobic
Uses oxygen		
Produces lactic acid		
Produces alcohol		
Releases the most energy		
Fermentation uses this type of respiration		

[5]

2 Anaerobic respiration in yeast is different to anaerobic respiration in humans. Describe the differences. [3]

3 Explain the importance of having a skeleton. [4]

4 Look at the diagram of the skeleton.

Complete the labels. [10]

5 Explain why each joint needs at least two different muscles. [3]

Looking at Plants and Ecosystems

1 Copy and complete the table by putting a tick (✔) in the correct box next to each statement about respiration and photosynthesis.

	Respiration	Photosynthesis
Produces oxygen		
Produces carbon dioxide		
Uses energy from sunlight		
Releases energy		
Requires chlorophyll		

[5]

2 Explain how a green leaf is adapted to perform photosynthesis. [5]

3 Complete this food web by adding arrows to show the flow of energy through the web. [7]

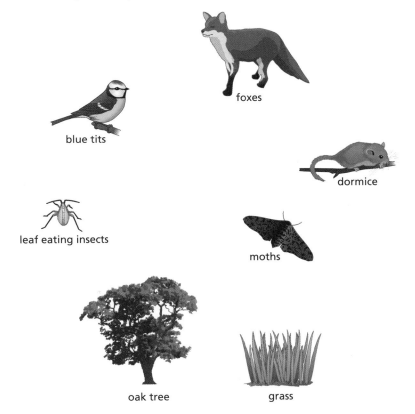

foxes

blue tits

dormice

leaf eating insects

moths

oak tree   grass

4 Explain why insects are so important in the production of food for humans. [2]

5 Poisonous substances sometimes get released into the environment. These poisons can be more dangerous to animals at the top of the food chain. Explain why. [2]

Variation for Survival

You must be able to:

- Explain how genetic information is inherited from our parents
- Understand the job of chromosomes and genes
- Know the contribution of different scientists to our understanding of DNA.

How Genetic Information is Inherited

- We inherit half our genetic information from our mother and half from our father. This is called **heredity**.
- The **inheritance** of genetic information happens when a sperm from the father fertilises an egg from the mother.

Fertilisation of egg

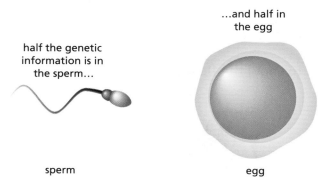

half the genetic information is in the sperm...

...and half in the egg

sperm

egg

> ### Key Point
>
> Half our genes come from our father and half from our mother. This is why we have similarities to both our mum and dad.

- The genetic information is stored on **chromosomes**, found in the nucleus of our cells.
- The nucleus of almost every cell in our body contains 46 chromosomes.
- However, sperm and eggs only contain 23 chromosomes.
- So 23 chromosomes come from our mother and 23 from our father.
- This produces new offspring with some features inherited from our mother and some from our father.

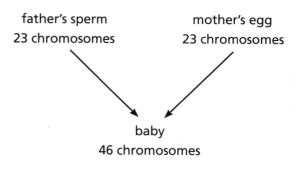

father's sperm
23 chromosomes

mother's egg
23 chromosomes

baby
46 chromosomes

- Each chromosome consists of a very long strand of **DNA**.
- The DNA is divided up into single units called **genes**.
- Each gene is a single section of DNA that codes for a protein.

From cell to gene

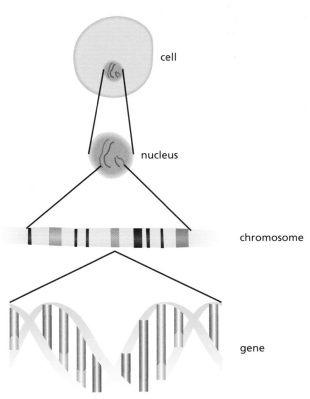

- cell
- nucleus
- chromosome
- gene

A gene

Famous Scientists and DNA

- Several different scientists played a part in discovering how genetic information is inherited.
- In 1953, James Watson and Francis Crick developed a theory for the structure of DNA.
- Maurice Wilkins helped produce evidence to support Watson and Crick's theory of the structure of DNA.
- Rosalind Franklin made X-ray images of DNA which showed that DNA was a double helix.
- Watson, Crick and Wilkins were awarded the Nobel prize for their work. Sadly, Franklin had died several years earlier and so could not be awarded the prize, even though her work was crucial to the discovery of DNA structure.

Quick Test

1. Where does a baby get its 46 chromosomes from?
2. Which is larger, a chromosome or a gene?
3. Write down what a gene is.
4. Name four scientists who were involved in the discovery of DNA.

Key Words

heredity
inheritance
chromosome
DNA
gene

Variation for Survival

You must be able to:

- Explain why variation within a species is so important
- Understand different types of variation
- Explain the effect of a changing environment on our survival.

Variation Between Species

- A species is a group of organisms that can reproduce to produce fertile offspring.
- All species are different. Scientists call this variation.
- Variation between species is called interspecific variation.

Variation Within a Species

- As well as variation between species, variation occurs *within* a species. This is called intraspecific variation.
- Apart from twins, all humans look different.
- Variation occurs because of sexual reproduction.
- Sexual reproduction mixes up the genes from mum and dad and this causes variation.
- Apart from identical twins, no two brothers or sisters will inherit the same combination of genes from their parents.

> **Key Point**
>
> Variation is due to different organisms having a different combination of genes.

Types of Variation

- There are two types of variation within a species: continuous variation and discontinuous variation.
- Height is an example of continuous variation. Some people are tall, others are short. But most people are somewhere in between.

- Blood groups are an example of discontinuous variation. People are either A, B, AB or O. There is no gradual range that goes from one to another.

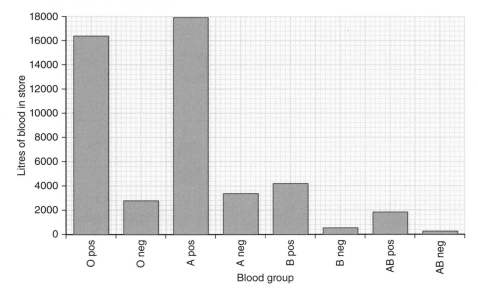

The Effect of a Changing Environment

- Variation is very important when the environment changes.
- Extinction of a species can happen when the environment changes. For example, global warming may cause some species to become extinct.
- This is because they are less able to compete for resources and reproduce in the changing environment.
- However, if the changes to the environment are small or occur slowly, because the members of a species are all slightly different some will be able to survive.
- These individuals survive and breed to produce new offspring, ensuring the survival of the species.
- This is why biodiversity is so important.
- The more biodiversity, the less likely it is that extinction will happen.

Gene Banks

- A gene bank is a place where scientists store seeds and cells from as many different organisms as possible.
- This helps to ensure that no genes are lost during extinction.
- These genes may be helpful in the future to provide new medicines or food.

Key Point

Biodiversity is a measure of the amount of variation between different organisms.

Key Words

species
fertile
variation
interspecific variation
intraspecific variation
continuous variation
discontinuous variation
extinction
biodiversity

Quick Test

1. Write down and explain two different types of variation.
2. Write down the main cause of variation in humans.
3. Explain the meaning of the word biodiversity.
4. What is a gene bank?

Our Health and the Effects of Drugs

You must be able to:

- Recall the four main types of drugs
- Describe legal and illegal recreational drugs and their effects
- Describe the dangers of smoking and drinking alcohol
- Understand drug addiction and withdrawal.

Main Types of Drugs

- A **drug** is a substance that affects the body in some way.
- There are many different drugs that affect the body in different ways.
- The four main types of drug are painkillers, depressants, stimulants and hallucinogens:

> **Key Point**
>
> Drugs can be used for medical or recreational reasons.

Type of drug	Effects	Examples	Dangers
Painkillers	Reduce pain and inflammation	Aspirin Paracetamol	Excess may damage stomach lining
Depressants	Make a person feel relaxed and drowsy	Cannabis	Drowsiness and lack of coordination; can cause post-use hallucinations
		Heroin	Reduces breathing and can cause death
Stimulants	Make a person feel energetic and alert	Cocaine Amphetamines	Can cause aggression and paranoia Can cause depression and panic
Hallucinogens	Make a person hear and see things more intensely	LSD	Confusion; users see and hear things that are not there
		Magic mushrooms	Can cause a bad trip; can cause flashbacks for some time afterwards

- All of these types of drug can be addictive.
- All drugs have **side-effects**.
- Side-effects are unwanted symptoms caused by taking the drug, e.g. rashes, headaches, or nausea.

Recreational Drugs

- Drugs that are taken for non-medical reasons are called **recreational drugs**.
- Some recreational drugs are legal and are in common use, for example, caffeine, tobacco, and alcohol.
- Some recreational drugs are illegal and can have dangerous side-effects, for example, cannabis, ecstasy and cocaine.

Smoking and Drinking Alcohol

- Two common recreational drugs are:
  - alcohol (found in alcoholic drinks such as wine and beer)
  - tobacco (found in cigarettes).
- People smoke cigarettes and drink alcohol as a way of relaxing and feeling more confident.
- Smoking and drinking too much alcohol carry serious health risks:

Smoking	Tobacco contains nicotine, a drug which speeds up heart rate and raises blood pressure, leading to increased risk of heart disease, heart attacks and strokes Smoking damages blood vessels and the lungs, leading to coughs, lung infections such as bronchitis, emphysema and lung cancer
Drinking alcohol	In the short term, alcohol: – slows down reactions – reduces coordination – can alter people's behaviour. In the long term, too much alcohol can cause: – liver failure – brain damage – increased risk of strokes and heart attacks – anxiety and depression

Addiction and Withdrawal

- **Addiction** to a drug means that when the person stops taking the drug, they suffer withdrawal symptoms.
- These symptoms may include sweating, shivering, headaches, muscle pain and sickness.

Key Words

drug
side-effect
recreational drug
addiction

Our Health and the Effects of Drugs

You must be able to:

- Explain how microbes can cause disease
- Describe how the body acts as a barrier to prevent disease
- Understand how bacteria, viruses and fungi cause disease
- Understand the importance of vaccination and antibiotics.

Microbes

- Microbes or microorganisms are very small organisms that can only be seen by using a microscope.
- Most microbes are harmless to humans but a small number of them can cause disease.

How Microbes Cause Disease

- Microbes can cause disease in one of two ways:
  1 They can attack and destroy cells in our body.
  2 They can produce chemicals called **toxins** that act like poisons in our body.
- Different types of microbes produce different types of diseases in our body.

How the Body Protects us from Disease

- Fortunately our body can protect us from some diseases. It can do this in several different ways.
- The skin acts as a barrier to stop the microbes entering the body.
- Microbes try to enter the body though body openings.

How the Blood Protects us Against Microbes

- Sometimes the skin gets damaged and microbes gain entry. We then need a different kind of defence against microbes.
- Our blood can clot to stop microbes from getting into the blood.
- Our blood contains white blood cells. These cells can attack and engulf microbes.

> **Key Point**
>
> Some microbes are even useful to humans, such as yeast used for bread and wine making.

> **Key Point**
>
> Microbes that cause disease are called **pathogens**.

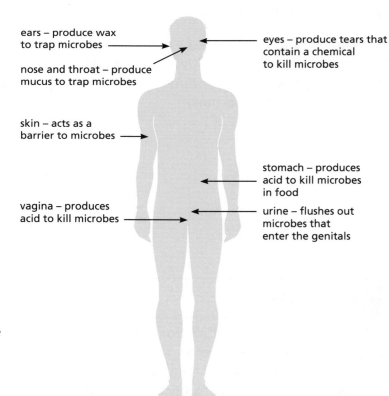

ears – produce wax to trap microbes

nose and throat – produce mucus to trap microbes

skin – acts as a barrier to microbes

vagina – produces acid to kill microbes

eyes – produce tears that contain a chemical to kill microbes

stomach – produces acid to kill microbes in food

urine – flushes out microbes that enter the genitals

- They can also make microbes clump together and produce chemicals to destroy them:

white blood cell

nucleus

pathogens

phagocytes ingest the pathogens

the pathogens are trapped

the pathogens have been digested

Key Point

White blood cells are part of a defence system called the immune system.

- There are some white blood cells called **memory cells**. When we get a disease that we recover from, our body makes memory cells. If the same microbe enters the body again the memory cells produce **antibodies** to destroy it even before we are aware of the fact that we are ill.

Bacteria, Viruses and Fungi

- There are three different types of microbes that can cause disease, **bacteria**, **viruses** and **fungi**.
- Bacteria can be seen with a light microscope and cause diseases such as tuberculosis.
- Viruses are much smaller and can only be seen with an electron microscope. They cause diseases such as polio.
- Fungi cause diseases such as athlete's foot.

Vaccines and Antibiotics

- Some diseases can be prevented by **vaccination** and some can be cured by **antibiotics**.
- Vaccination is when dead microbes are injected into the body causing the blood to make memory cells. We are then protected against that microbe.
- Antibiotics are chemicals which kill bacteria that have entered our body.

Key Point

Antibiotics do not work against viruses.

Key Words

toxins
pathogen
memory cell
antibodies
bacteria
virus
fungi
vaccination
antibiotic

Quick Test

1. Describe three ways our body stops microbes from entering.
2. Name three different types of microbes.
3. Explain what is meant by vaccination.
4. Explain why doctors do not prescribe antibiotics for infections caused by a virus.

Getting the Energy your Body Needs

1 Copy the table below and draw a straight line from each description of respiration, to the correct type of respiration.

Type of respiration   **Description of respiration**   **Type of respiration**

Uses oxygen

Produces lactic acid

Aerobic

Anaerobic

Produces alcohol

Releases the least amount of energy

[4]

2 Complete the following word equations:

a) for aerobic respiration

oxygen + _____ → water + _____ + energy   [2]

b) for fermentation in yeast

glucose → _____ + _____ + energy   [2]

c) for anaerobic respiration in humans

glucose → _____ + energy   [1]

3 Explain why respiration in living organisms is so important.   [2]

4 The skeleton is an important structure.

Copy the table and put a tick (✓) in the boxes next to each function performed by the skeleton.

Carries oxygen around the body	
Supports the body	
Helps with movement	
Where food is digested	
Protects some organs	
Makes red blood cells	
Where anaerobic respiration takes place	

[4]

5 Joints allow the skeleton to move. Identify the structures numbered 1–5 in the diagram of the knee joint. [5]

6 Look at the diagram of the human arm.

a) Explain the job done by organ **A**. [2]

b) Explain the job done by organ **B**. [2]

c) What single word best describes these two organs? [1]

Looking at Plants and Ecosystems

1 a) Complete this word equation for photosynthesis:

water + _____ → glucose + _____ [2]

b) Write down two other things needed for photosynthesis to take place. [2]

2 Using the two gases, carbon dioxide and oxygen, show how animals and plants are dependent upon each other. [4]

Variation for Survival

1. Copy and complete the table below by writing down in each box the correct number of chromosomes found in the nucleus of these types of human cell.

Cell	Number of chromosomes
Muscle cell	
Nerve cell	
Sperm cell	
Egg cell	
Embryo cell	

[5]

2. Give the correct labels for **A** to **D** on the diagram. Choose from the words given below. [4]

nucleus	cell	gene	chromosome

A

B

C

D

3 The graph shows variation of a characteristic found in humans. Variation can be either continuous or discontinuous.

Use the graph to explain the differences between these two types of variation. [2]

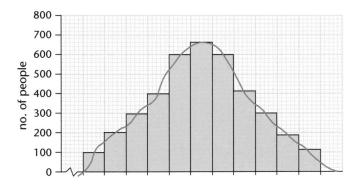

Our Health and the Effects of Drugs

1 Look at the outline drawing of the human body.

Add labels to the drawing to show how the body prevents the entry of microbes. [7]

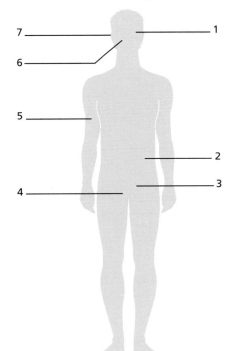

2 Explain the difference between a medical drug and a recreational drug. [2]

3 Recreational drugs can be divided into three categories: depressants, stimulants and hallucinogens. Give one example of each type of drug and describe its effects on the human body. [6]

4 Many people drink alcohol excessively and smoke. Describe the possible long-term effects on the human body of drinking alcohol excessively and smoking. [5]

Mixing, Dissolving and Separating

You must be able to:

- Represent pure substances and mixtures using simple particle pictures
- Demonstrate a range of laboratory skills
- Apply appropriate separation techniques to different mixtures.

Pure and Impure Substances

- In chemistry a 'pure' substance is one that contains only one type of atom or compound.
- An impure substance contains more than one substance (element or compound), forming a mixture.
- The substances in the mixture are not chemically joined together so it should be easy to separate them.
- A common example of a mixture is sugar dissolved in water.

Particle diagram of sugar dissolved in water

Water molecules in a pure solution

A sugar solution with water and sugar molecules

Chromatography

- Chromatography separates dissolved pigments in solution, e.g. the pigments in ink:

  1 The sample mixture is loaded on a pre-marked line at the bottom of a piece of chromatography paper and dipped into solvent.

  2 As the **solvent** moves up the paper it takes the dissolved pigments with it.

  3 Since the pigments have different solubilities they travel at different speeds and so separate.

  4 The most soluble pigments move the furthest; less soluble pigments move less far.

Chromatography

most soluble

least soluble

Key Point

A pencil line marks the starting point as it will not move with the ink pigments.

Filtering

- **Filtration** separates an insoluble solid from a liquid by passing the solid/liquid mixture through filter paper.
- The **filtrate** is the liquid which passes through the filter paper and the solid left behind is the residue.
- Excess copper oxide in copper sulfate solution can be separated by filtration. Copper sulfate is the filtrate, copper oxide is the residue.

filter paper

mixture

filter funnel

copper oxide (residue)

beaker

copper sulfate (filtrate)

Evaporation

- **Evaporation** is used to remove the liquid part of a mixture and collect the dissolved solid.
- The mixture is placed in a suitable container (e.g. a watch glass) and heated, sometimes by using a Bunsen burner.

Distillation

- Liquids have different boiling points.
- By carefully controlling the temperature of a heated mixture of two or more liquids, the liquids evaporate at different times. This is known as distillation.
- The evaporated gas is cooled back into liquid and collected as **distillate** in a collecting vessel.
- The fragrances used in perfumes are separated by distillation, as well as the different parts of crude oil.

Distillation of ethanol (an alcohol) and water mixture

- thermometer
- condenser
- distillation flask
- cooling water out
- cooling water in
- alcohol/water mixture
- HEAT
- pure alcohol (distillate)

1 The mixture is heated until the liquid with the lowest boiling point boils.

2 The thermometer measures the temperature of the gas.

3 The water in the condenser cools the gas, allowing it to condense back into a liquid.

4 The liquid (distillate) is collected.

Revise

Key Point

The slower the liquid evaporates, the larger the crystals that form.

Quick Test

1. How could you separate an insoluble solid from a liquid?
2. What size crystals are made from rapid evaporation?
3. What does 'distillate' mean?
4. Describe how to carry out chromatography.

Key Words

solvent
filtration
filtrate
evaporation
distillate

Mixing, Dissolving and Separating

You must be able to:

- Explain the conservation of mass in reactions and changes of state
- Represent pure substances and mixtures using particle pictures and word equations
- Explain similarities and differences between combustion, thermal decomposition, oxidation and reduction.

Conservation of Mass

- The law of conservation of mass states that in any physical change or chemical reaction the mass after the change will be the same as the mass before the change.
- With state changes this means that the number of particles of the substance at the start will equal the number of particles at the end.

Conservation of mass

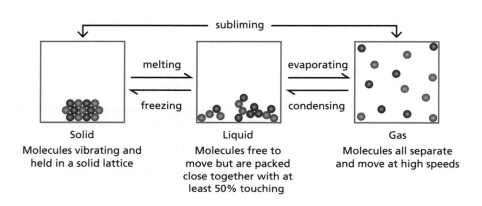

Solid	Liquid	Gas
Molecules vibrating and held in a solid lattice	Molecules free to move but are packed close together with at least 50% touching	Molecules all separate and move at high speeds

> **Key Point**
>
> When drawing a particle diagram for a liquid at least half of the particles should be touching each other.

- With a chemical reaction the atoms of the reactants are rearranged to form the products. Atoms cannot 'disappear'.

Combustion

- **Combustion** is the reaction between a fuel and oxygen.
- Carbon dioxide and water are generally produced as waste products when the fuel is a hydrocarbon.
- Energy is released as heat and light.

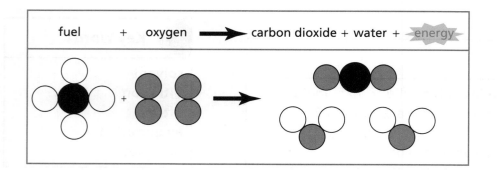

fuel + oxygen ⟶ carbon dioxide + water + energy

> **Key Point**
>
> Energy has not been made, it has just been released.

Thermal Decomposition

- Some compounds break down into new molecules when heated; they don't react with oxygen in the air.
- This is called **thermal decomposition**.
- An example is chalk, which has the chemical name calcium carbonate.

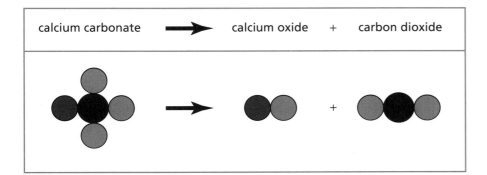

| calcium carbonate | ⟶ | calcium oxide | + | carbon dioxide |

Oxidation and Reduction

- When substances gain oxygen in a reaction it is called **oxidation**.
- Losing oxygen in a reaction is called **reduction**.
- For example, carbon can be oxidized to form carbon dioxide:

Oxidation forming rust

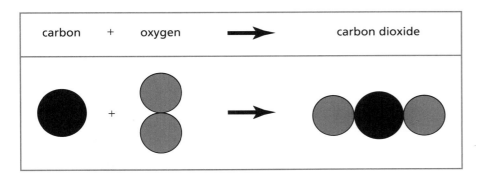

| carbon | + | oxygen | ⟶ | carbon dioxide |

- The reaction of iron with water and oxygen is a special form of oxidation, forming iron (III) oxide, which is known as **rust.**

iron + water + oxygen ⟶ hydrated iron (III) oxide

- Rusting requires oxygen and water. It happens faster when salt is dissolved in the water.

Quick Test

1. Draw diagrams to show the atoms in a solid, liquid and gas.
2. Describe how calcium carbonate thermally decomposes.
3. What is meant by the term oxidation?
4. What does iron have to react with in order to rust?

Elements, Compounds and Reactions

You must be able to:

- Explain the structure of the periodic table, including groups, periods, symbols and formulae
- Explain differences between elements and compounds in terms of particles
- Describe the differences between physical changes and chemical reactions.

The Periodic Table

- The periodic table contains all the **elements** that are found in the universe.
- An element is a substance that contains only identical atoms.
- The simplest particle of an element that cannot be broken down further without losing its properties is called an **atom**.
- The periodic table arranges the elements based on the atomic number (the number of protons in the nucleus of each atom) and the physical and chemical properties of each element.
- Each column of the periodic table is called a **group**, a family of elements with similar physical and chemical properties.
- The rows in the periodic table are called **periods**. The atomic number increases from left to right through the period.
- The majority of elements in the periodic table are metals; the non-metals are less common.

Key Point

The atomic number of elements increases sequentially in whole numbers as you go through the table.

Key

■ Metals

■ Non-metals

- The periodic table used today was devised by the Russian chemist Dmitri Mendeleev.
- We can use the periodic table to predict the physical and chemical properties of elements.

- For example, elements in a group are very similar. They have similar physical properties and chemical reactions:
  - The metals in group 1 all react with water to form alkaline solutions
  - The non-metals in group 7 are good at killing bacteria.

Chemical Symbols and Formulae

- Elements have a name and a chemical symbol.
- Normally this is one or two letters, for example Helium = He, Copper = Cu, Silver = Ag.
- When chemicals react and chemically join together they form compounds.
- The compound is represented by a chemical formula, e.g. water = H_2O, where two hydrogen atoms are joined to one oxygen atom.
- The number written as a subscript indicates how many of those atoms are in the compound, e.g. $C_6H_{12}O_6$ (glucose) contains 6 carbon, 12 hydrogen and 6 oxygen atoms.

> **Key Point**
>
> Take care to write only the first letter of an element's symbol as a capital letter.

Physical Changes and Chemical Reactions

- A physical change is where a substance changes state, e.g. water (liquid) freezing into ice (solid).
- Physical changes are easy to reverse.
- A chemical reaction is where elements chemically join together to form a compound.
- It is difficult to reverse a chemical reaction.
- The compound formed has different properties to those of the original elements.
- To make it clear what is happening in a reaction we write a chemical equation:
  - On the left hand side we write the **reactants**
  - On the right hand side we write the **products** formed.
- An example is the reaction of sodium with chlorine:

on the right left hand side we write the reactants on the right hand side we write the product formed

> **Quick Test**
>
> 1. Which of the following are compounds?
> O_2 CO_2 H_2O
> 2. What is the atomic number of an element?
> 3. How many hydrogen atoms are in H_2SO_4?
> 4. How many different elements make up $C_6H_{12}O_6$?

> **Key Words**
>
> element
> atom
> group
> period
> reactant
> product

Elements, Compounds and Reactions

You must be able to:

- Describe the properties of metals and non-metals
- Explain the reactions of metals and metal oxides with acids
- Understand the concept of a reaction using oxidation of metals and non-metals.

Properties of Metals and Non-metals

Metal – copper wires used to conduct electricity

Metals	Non-metals
Conduct electricity and heat	Are unable to conduct electricity and heat
Are **ductile** (can be drawn into wires)	Often have a low melting point and boiling point
Are **malleable** (can be hammered into shape)	Are often gases at room temperature
Are shiny	Often have a lower **density** than metals.
Are sonorous (ring like a bell when hit)	
Often have a high melting point and boiling point.	

Non-metal – helium gas used to inflate balloons

Reactions of Metals

- Metals react with acids to give a **salt** and hydrogen:

> **metal + acid ⟶ salt + hydrogen**

- The salt formed always takes the name of the metal plus a suffix that represents the acid used in the reaction:

Acid	Suffix	Example
Hydrochloric acid	Chloride	**sodium + hydrochloric acid ⟶ sodium chloride + hydrogen**
Sulfuric acid	Sulfate	**sodium + sulfuric acid ⟶ sodium sulfate + hydrogen**
Nitric acid	Nitrate	**sodium + nitric acid ⟶ sodium nitrate + hydrogen**
Phosphoric acid	Phosphate	**sodium + phosphoric acid ⟶ sodium phosphate + hydrogen**

Oxidation

- Reacting an element or compound with oxygen is called oxidation.
- The atoms that make up the elements and compounds rearrange to make a new compound, an oxide. For example:

> magnesium + oxygen ⟶ magnesium oxide

- This can also be written as a balanced equation.
- A balanced equation indicates the number of atoms and how they are arranged.
- For example, two atoms of magnesium react with one molecule of oxygen to form two molecules of magnesium oxide:

> $2Mg(s) + O_2(g) \longrightarrow 2MgO(s)$

- Combustion is where a fuel reacts with oxygen (burns) forming carbon dioxide and water, and giving out energy in the process:

> fuel + oxygen ⟶ carbon dioxide + water + energy

Key Point

The numbers of each atom are always the same on both sides of the formula.

Reactions of Metal Oxides

- Metals react with oxygen to form metal oxides, for example:

> magnesium + oxygen ⟶ magnesium oxide

- The metal oxide is called a base and is the chemical opposite of an acid.
- Metal oxides react with acids to form a salt and water:

> metal oxide + acid ⟶ salt + water

- This means that the acid has been neutralised.
- The salt formed always takes the name of the metal and the suffix from the acid, for example:

> sodium oxide + hydrochloric acid ⟶ sodium chloride + water

Salt

Quick Test

1. Write the word equation for the reaction between nitrogen and oxygen.
2. What salt is formed in the reaction between potassium and sulfuric acid?
3. Give three properties of a metal.
4. Give three properties of a non-metal.

Key Words

ductile
malleable
density
salt
oxidation
base
neutralise

Revise

Variation for Survival

1 The graph shows variation of a characteristic found in humans.

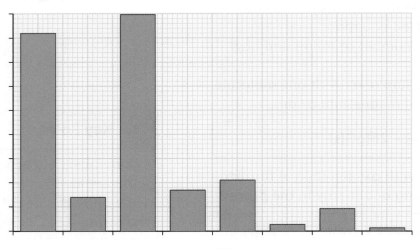

a) What is the name of this type of variation? [1]

b) Write down two examples of this type of variation found in humans. [2]

2 Variation is very important to the survival of a species.

Under which of the following conditions is variation most important? Put a tick next to the best answer from the table below.

When environmental conditions stay the same	
When the environment is changing very slowly	
When the environment is changing very quickly	
The environment has no effect on variation	

[1]

3 Explain the part played by each of the following scientists in the understanding of DNA.

a) Watson and Crick. [1]

b) Rosalind Franklin. [1]

Our Health and the Effects of Drugs

1 Explain the meaning of the following words:

   a) pathogen

   b) toxin

   c) antibody   [3]

2 Name three different types of microbe and give an example of a disease caused
   by each of them.   [3]

3 Explain why doctors are less worried about people taking the drug caffeine and more worried
   about people taking the drug cocaine.   [2]

4 Explain the difference between addiction and withdrawal.   [2]

5 Match each activity below with a danger of doing it.

Activity		Danger
Drinking alcohol		Trying to fly off a tall building
Smoking		Reduces breathing
Taking LSD		Lung cancer
Using heroin		Liver failure

[4]

6 Microbes sometimes gain entry to our body.

   Explain how white blood cells can protect our body from invasion by microbes.   [3]

Mixing, Dissolving and Separating

1 Which of the following separation methods would be best for each of the following investigations?

Choose from the following methods:

chromatography　　　　　　**distillation**　　　　　　**filtration**

a) Extracting alcohol from beer. [1]

b) Checking whether a note written in blue ink was written using a particular pen. [1]

c) Separating sand from a mixture of sand and water. [1]

2 a) Which two of the following diagrams show a pure substance? [2]

A	B	C	D

b) Which of the substances could be copper? [1]

3 Describe how filtration and evaporation could be used to extract salt from seawater. [5]

4 Vinnie is analysing the pigments used to colour different sweets using chromatography.

Vinnie makes a qualitative observation on how similar the chromatograms are to each other using his eyes and judgement.

Suggest what Vinnie would need to do to make a more accurate quantitative measurement. [2]

5 An aquarium for keeping fish uses a filter.

Suggest what the filter is removing from the water and explain how filtration works. [3]

Elements, Compounds and Reactions

1 Ethan is painting a model. When he opens a tin of paint he notices that the paint has separated into layers.

   a) What type of a substance is the paint?

     i) an element   **ii)** a compound   **iii)** a mixture   [1]

   b) When Ethan reads the label on the tin it says that the paint contains water and titanium oxide. Titanium oxide and water are examples of what type of substance?

     i) an element   **ii)** a compound   **iii)** a mixture   [1]

2 Which of the following are examples of chemical reactions?

   i) chocolate melting on a hot day

   ii) a firework exploding in the sky

   iii) bread being toasted

   iv) water condensing on a cold window pane   [2]

3 A periodic table is shown below.

   a) Which letter indicates a group?   [1]

   b) Which letter indicates a period?   [1]

   c) Which letter indicates a non-metal?   [1]

4 Explain the difference between an element and a compound.   [3]

Explaining Physical Changes

You must be able to:

- Describe the similarities and differences between solids, liquids and gases
- Explain how changes in temperature affect the motion and spacing of particles
- Explain sublimation in terms of particles.

The Particulate Nature of Matter

- All matter in the universe is made up of **atoms**, arranged in one of three states: solid, liquid or gas.
- At the coldest temperature possible (–273 °C or 0 K), the atoms have no **kinetic energy** so cannot move.
- If heat is introduced, the atoms gain kinetic energy and so move.

Solid

Solids, Liquids and Gases

- Solids:
  - contain atoms arranged as close together as possible
  - are therefore denser than their liquid form (apart from water) and cannot be compressed
  - will have a fixed shape and volume that does not depend upon the container that it is in.
- Even though they form part of a solid the atoms, or molecules, still vibrate due to their kinetic energy.
- As the temperature supplied to a substance increases, the atoms or molecules vibrate more and more.
- Eventually, at the melting point, the atoms or molecules rearrange into a liquid:
  - as the atoms or molecules are further apart the **density** will be less than it was as a solid
  - if a liquid is in a container it will take the shape of the container that it occupies
  - the atoms or molecules move around much more than in a solid, but still cannot be compressed.
- Eventually, at the boiling point, the liquid becomes a gas:
  - the atoms or molecules in a gas can move freely and will occupy all of the available space in a container
  - if not completely enclosed, the gas particles will escape
  - when a material cools, the reverse process happens.
- Unlike solids and liquids, gases can be compressed.
- Kinetic energy is removed from the substance, causing its movement to slow.
- The substance changes from a gas into a liquid (condenses), then into a solid from a liquid (freezing).

Liquid

Gas

Key Point

Gases can still be heated further, to temperatures higher than the boiling point.

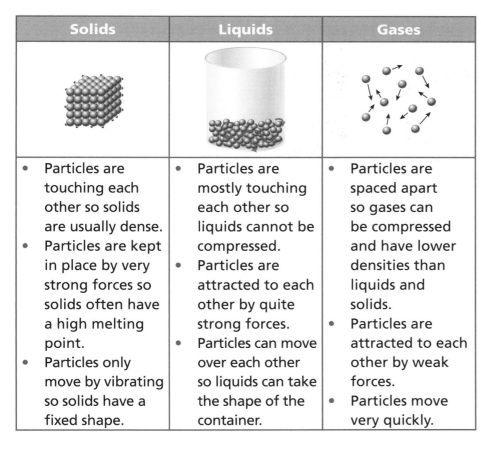

Solids	Liquids	Gases
• Particles are touching each other so solids are usually dense. • Particles are kept in place by very strong forces so solids often have a high melting point. • Particles only move by vibrating so solids have a fixed shape.	• Particles are mostly touching each other so liquids cannot be compressed. • Particles are attracted to each other by quite strong forces. • Particles can move over each other so liquids can take the shape of the container.	• Particles are spaced apart so gases can be compressed and have lower densities than liquids and solids. • Particles are attracted to each other by weak forces. • Particles move very quickly.

Sublimation

- Some substances can jump from solid to gas. This is called sublimation.
- Examples of sublimation include carbon dioxide (dry ice to gas), ammonium chloride and gel air freshener.

Sublimation

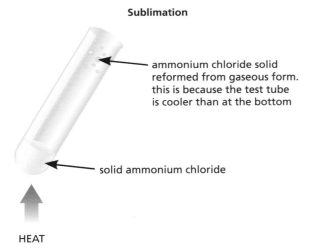

ammonium chloride solid reformed from gaseous form. this is because the test tube is cooler than at the bottom

solid ammonium chloride

HEAT

Gel air freshener

Quick Test

1. Why are most solids denser than their liquid form?
2. At what temperature do atoms stop vibrating?
3. Describe what happens in sublimation.
4. State the differences between solids, liquids and gases.

Key Words

atom
kinetic energy
density
sublimation

Explaining Physical Changes

You must be able to:

- Describe the particular nature of water and the ice/water transition
- Describe and explain Brownian motion and the diffusion of gases
- Explain the process of heat conduction between particles in a conductor.

Water

- Water has a number of properties that are unique.
- When ice forms, the water molecules line up in a regular pattern.
- The water molecules are further apart in ice than in the liquid form, and therefore solid water is less dense than liquid water.
- Consequently, ice floats on water.

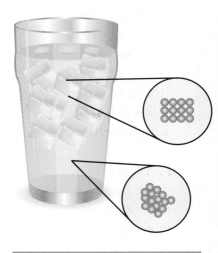

Brownian Motion

- In the 1800s Robert Brown observed pollen grains suspended in water under the microscope.
- He noticed that the particles were moving randomly in the water, and his observation is now called Brownian motion.
- Brownian motion is due to the particles suspended in a fluid colliding with the atoms or molecules that make up the fluid.

Key Point

The particle appears to move on its own, this is because the water molecules are so small that they are invisible.

Diffusion

- Diffusion is the name of the process whereby molecules in a liquid or gas mix as a result of their random motion.
- Particles at a high concentration in one location will tend to move to an area where they are in low concentration.
- Eventually the particles will become evenly distributed throughout the liquid or gas.

Conduction

- When a solid conductor, such as metal, is heated, the atoms increase their energy and vibrate more.
- The atoms collide with other atoms, transferring energy and causing them to vibrate more.
- The process of conduction continues until all the atoms have reached the same temperature.
- In an insulator the energy is not passed onto other atoms so the solid does not conduct the heat.
- The vibration of the particles increases as their kinetic energy increases.
- The higher the temperature, the greater the kinetic energy and so the particles vibrate faster.
- The lower the temperature, the lower the kinetic energy and the particles will vibrate more slowly.

Key Point

Kinetic energy is movement energy. The more movement, the more energy.

Temperature and Particles

- The hotter particles get, the more kinetic energy they have.
- This means particles move more and separate from each other more.
- As temperature increases, pressure will increase and the density will decrease.
- In the case of a balloon, the particles inside will increase in speed causing the pressure to increase, enlarging the balloon.

Movement of particles inside a warmed balloon

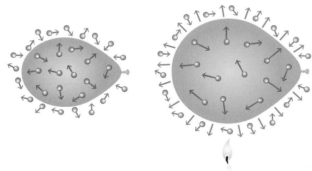

gas pressure depends on both density and temperature

heating the air also increases the pressure

- A reaction that produces heat energy is called an exothermic reaction.
- A reaction that takes in energy from the environment is called an endothermic reaction.

Quick Test

1. What will happen to the air particles in a sealed balloon if it is heated?
2. What will happen to the air particles in a sealed balloon if it is cooled?
3. Why does ice float on water?
4. Explain how diffusion takes place.

Key Words

Brownian motion
diffusion
concentration
pressure

Explaining Chemical Changes

You must be able to:

- Apply conservation of mass to simple reactions
- Explain the combustion of fuels
- Explain the difference between a chemical and physical change
- Explain how a catalyst can make a reaction occur faster by reducing activation energy.

Chemical Reactions

- A chemical reaction involves the rearrangement of atoms from reactants to products.
- The products that are formed have the same atoms, just in different configurations.
- There is never a change in total mass in a chemical reaction.
- A **word equation** names the reactants and products formed in a reaction, for example:

reactants $\longrightarrow$ product
hydrogen + oxygen $\longrightarrow$ water

> **Key Point**
>
> The total mass in a chemical reaction doesn't change. This is conservation of mass.

- Word equations do not tell us the ratios of the molecules involved.
- **Chemical equations** show the chemical formula of the reactants and products, so that the number of atoms and ratios involved can be worked out, for example:

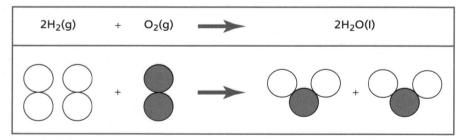

$$2H_2(g) \quad + \quad O_2(g) \quad \longrightarrow \quad 2H_2O(l)$$

> **Key Point**
>
> The large number in front of each molecule is a coefficient. It tells us how many molecules there are overall.

- This equation tells us that two molecules of hydrogen gas react with one molecule of oxygen gas to give two molecules of water.
- The state of each reactant is given in brackets after its chemical formula: (s) = solid, (g) = gas, (l) = liquid, (aq) = aqueous (which means it is in solution).
- In combustion, a fuel generally reacts with oxygen to produce carbon dioxide and water, and releases energy in the process. For example, burning propane gas in a camping stove:

propane + oxygen $\longrightarrow$ carbon dioxide + water (+ energy)
$C_3H_8(g) + 5O_2(g) \longrightarrow \quad 3CO_2(g) \quad + 4H_2O(l)$

Catalysts

- A chemical reaction will only take place if a set amount of energy is provided.
- This is called the **activation energy** of the reaction.
- If the available energy is less than the activation energy, there will not be a reaction.
- A **catalyst** is a substance that reduces the activation energy, and so increases the rate of reaction.
- This means the reaction can take place with lower energy than normal.
- A catalyst is neither a reactant nor a product and is not used up in the reaction.
- The name of the catalyst is written above the arrow in the reaction to indicate that it is needed.
- Catalysts are used in chemical processes all over the world, most commonly in the exhaust systems of cars.

> **Key Point**
>
> Catalysts are never used up, so can be used again and again.

Catalytic convertor

clean gases out

polluted gases in

Pt catalyst to catalyse
the breakdown of pollutants

Pt catalyst
carbon monoxide + oxygen ⟶ carbon dioxide
Pt catalyst
$2CO(g)$ + $O_2(g)$ ⟶ $2CO_2(g)$

- In biology, catalysts are made of protein and are called enzymes.
- One example of an enzyme is amylase in the digestion of starch into the sugar maltose:

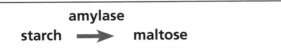

amylase
starch ⟶ maltose

> **Quick Test**
>
> 1. What does a catalyst do?
> 2. Explain activation energy.
> 3. State the differences between word and chemical equations.
> 4. Write the four state symbols used in equations.

> **Key Words**
>
> word equation
> chemical equation
> activation energy
> catalyst

Explaining Chemical Changes

You must be able to:

- Explain neutralisation and the use of indicators
- Use word equations to represent and/or describe the reactions of acids
- Describe and explain the uses of acids and alkalis.

Indicators

- Indicators are used to find out what type of substance a chemical is.
- Initially, scientists discovered chemicals in common plants that could change colour to indicate acid or alkali, for example, red cabbage is red in acid and blue in alkaline conditions.
- The chemical litmus also behaves as an indicator but can be incorporated into paper, so it can be transported easily.
- Universal indicator (UI) solution and paper contain a mixture of different indicators.
- These indicators change colour at a specific pH.
- pH is a measure of the strength of an acid or alkali.
- The pH scale ranges from 1 to 14 and has a colour for each pH number.

Litmus paper

- pH probes and data loggers remove the need for indicator papers and solutions.
- They measure the pH directly and are more precise than indicator papers or solutions.

Acids and Bases

- All chemicals can be classified as being an acid, a base or are neutral.
- Acids are a group of chemicals that have a pH less than 7.
- An acid can chemically react with a metal to produce hydrogen:

metal + acid ⟶ salt + hydrogen

- The chemical opposite of an acid is a base.
- Bases are chemicals with a pH greater than 7.

> **Key Point**
>
> If a base dissolves, it's an alkali.

Name of acid	Where found	pH
Hydrochloric acid	Human stomach	1
Ethanoic acid	Vinegar	2
Citric acid	Citrus fruit	2
Sulfuric acid	Car batteries	1
Carbonic acid	Fizzy drinks	4

Name of base	Where found	pH
Sodium hydroxide	Laboratories	14
Calcium carbonate	Chalk	9
Sodium bicarbonate	Bicarbonate of soda (cooking)	8
Ammonia	Hair dyes	11
Lime	Gardening products	12

Citrus fruit – acid

Chalk – base

- When a chemical is neither an acid nor a base it is neutral.
- A neutral solution has a pH of 7.

Neutralisation

- When an acid and a base are mixed together, they react.
- If an acid is reacted with a base there will come a point where a salt and water are made and no more acid or base exists.
- At this point the mixture will be neutral and have a pH of 7.
- The whole process is called neutralisation.

acid + metal oxide ⟶ salt + water
acid + metal hydroxide ⟶ salt + water
acid + metal carbonates ⟶ salt + water + carbon dioxide

Key Point

In all neutralisation reactions, water is made.

Quick Test

1. What can you deduce if a chemical is pH 5?
2. Explain neutralisation.
3. Write the word equation for the reaction of acid and metal.
4. Why is a pH probe and a data logger better to measure pH than UI paper?

Key Words

acid
base
neutral
alkali
neutralisation

Mixing, Dissolving and Separating

1 Anna and Kala are carrying out chromatography of ink, as they believe a cheque has been forged. They are going to test to see whether the ink on the cheque is the same as the ink of the suspect's pen. The results are shown in the chromatogram below.

A   B   C   D   Suspect's pen

a) How many different pigments are in sample A and in sample B? [2]

b) Which of the samples matches the ink of the suspect's pen? [1]

c) Explain why was the starting line on the chromatogram was drawn using a pencil. [2]

2 Karim is investigating how chalk (calcium carbonate) reacts when heated. He heats the chalk for a minute at a time and then measures its mass.

He notices that the mass decreases.

a) What is the name given to the chemical reaction Karim is observing? [1]

b) Complete the word equation for the reaction given below:

    calcium carbonate → _____ + _____ [2]

3 Write the chemical equation for the reaction of carbon with oxygen. [3]

Elements, Compounds and Reactions

1 The diagram shows a model of a chemical reaction.

a) What feature of the diagram indicates that a chemical reaction has taken place? [2]

b) Substance X is oxygen. Suggest what substances Y and Z could be. [2]

c) Suggest how the diagram indicates that mass has been conserved in the reaction. [1]

substance X + substance Y → substance Z

2 Niamh is carrying out some experiments to observe what happens when different metals are added to different acids.

Her table has some gaps. What are the reactants and products given by letters A–E?

Metal	Name of acid	Salt formed	Gas formed
Zinc	A	Zinc sulfate	Hydrogen
Magnesium	Nitric acid	B	Hydrogen
Potassium	C	Potassium chloride	D
E	Nitric acid	Lithium nitrate	Hydrogen

[4]

3 For each change given below, decide whether it is a physical change (P) or a chemical change (C).

a) melting chocolate

b) a burning firework

c) the smell of perfume diffusing across a room

d) jelly setting in a dish

e) setting off a CO_2 fire extinguisher [1]

4 Which of the following chemical equations is correct?

a) $Mg(s) + O_2(g) \rightarrow 2MgO(s)$

b) $2Mg(s) + O(g) \rightarrow MgO(s)$

c) $2Mg(s) + O_2(g) \rightarrow 2MgO(s)$

d) $Mg(s) + O(g) \rightarrow MgO(s)$ [1]

Explaining Physical Changes

1. Draw the particles in a solid, liquid and a gas. [3]

2. Sally is looking at a blue coloured gel air freshener, which sublimes. She cuts a piece of the air freshener and puts it into a small beaker. The beaker is placed into a larger beaker which contains hot water. On the top of the beaker containing air freshener, she places a beaker containing ice.

   a) What would Sally see after a few minutes on the underside of the beaker containing ice? [1]

   b) Suggest why this happens. [1]

3. What is meant by the term Brownian motion? [2]

4. An iceberg floats on water. Explain what properties of water enable ice to float. [3]

5. Claude is holding a CO_2 fire extinguisher. When he sets the extinguisher off, a valve opens releasing CO_2 gas.

   When a handkerchief is placed over the end of the extinguisher, solid CO_2 starts to build up.

   Which of the following best explains why this happens? Tick the correct box.

   a) The CO_2 particles break up into C and O_2 ☐

   b) The CO_2 gas particles are slowed down rapidly causing a solid to form ☐

   c) The CO_2 gas particles slow down to form a liquid and then a solid ☐

   d) The handkerchief cools the CO_2 down into a solid ☐ [1]

Explaining Chemical Changes

1   Mark is reacting copper metal with oxygen gas. He draws the atoms involved in the reaction.

Cu atoms   O$_2$ atoms

   a) Draw what should be in the last box.   [2]

   b) What is the name of the product in this reaction?   [1]

2   What does a catalyst do in a chemical reaction? Choose the best answer.

   a) It slows a chemical reaction down

   b) It makes chemical reactions happen

   c) It lowers the activation energy

   d) It lowers the kinetic energy   [1]

3   Complete the following:

   metal + acid → _____ + _____   [1]

4   Peter is using universal indicator to identify acids and bases.

   Suggest what colour UI would change to for each of the examples below:

   a) car battery acid

   b) juice of a lemon

   c) tap water

   d) toothpaste   [4]

5   What are the products of the following reactions?

   a) magnesium + hydrochloric acid   →   [1]

   b) copper oxide + nitric acid   →   [1]

   c) vanadium carbonate + sulfuric acid   →   [1]

Obtaining Useful Materials

You must be able to:

- Use the reactivity series to determine whether reactions are possible
- Describe and explain how carbon is used to extract metals.

The Reactivity Series

- The metals in the periodic table all exhibit different levels of reactivity.
- By comparing their reactions it is possible to sort them into a reactivity series.
- The reactivity series shows the order of reactivity, from most reactive to least reactive.

Most reactive

Potassium

Sodium

Calcium

Magnesium

Aluminium

Carbon

Zinc

Iron

Tin

Lead

Copper

Silver

Gold

Platinum

Least reactive

> **Key Point**
>
> All metals could be included in a reactivity series. The diagram here shows only a few major metals, as well as carbon.

Structure of diamond
Diamond is very strong

- By comparing metals on the reactivity series, chemists can predict whether a chemical reaction may happen and, if it does, how vigorous the reaction may be.
- The reactivity series also includes the element carbon.
- Carbon can have different forms and properties, such as diamond and graphite.
- Carbon is not a metal, but when it is in the form of graphite it can conduct electricity, a property shared with the metals.

Structure of graphite
Graphite conducts electricity

Displacement Reactions

- When a metal, or carbon, comes into contact with a metal that is in a compound there may be a reaction:
  - If the metal in the compound is higher in the reactivity series than the introduced metal, or carbon, no reaction will take place.
  - If the metal in the compound is lower in the reactivity series than the introduced metal or carbon then the introduced metal will **displace** the metal in the compound.
  - The greater the difference in positions in the reactivity series, the faster and more vigorous the reaction.
- For example, if iron metal was added to copper sulfate solution:

Key Point

Remember that, as well as new products being formed, there will often be visible changes as a result of the reactants disappearing.

Iron nail in copper sulfate solution

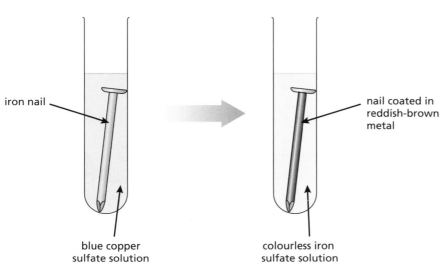

iron nail

nail coated in reddish-brown metal

blue copper sulfate solution

colourless iron sulfate solution

Iron is higher than copper on the reactivity series. It will therefore displace the copper and form iron sulfate. Iron is a silver coloured metal. It will slowly dissolve. The blue copper sulfate solution will lose its colour as the copper is displaced and colourless iron sulfate is formed. The copper, which was previously in solution, will form a reddish-brown solid.

- The reaction can be written as:

iron + copper sulfate $\longrightarrow$ iron sulfate + copper
$Fe(s) + CuSO_4(aq) \longrightarrow FeSO_4(aq) + Cu(s)$

- If copper were added to iron sulfate solution, there would be no reaction as copper is lower in the reactivity series than iron and will not be able to displace it.

Quick Test

1. Could copper displace magnesium from magnesium nitrate?
2. Which would be faster at displacing zinc – iron or aluminium?
3. Suggest a metal to displace sodium from sodium chloride.
4. Explain what is meant by the 'reactivity series'.

Key Words

reactivity
displace

Obtaining Useful Materials

You must be able to:

- Describe and explain the use of carbon in the extraction of metals
- Describe the characteristics and uses of ceramics, composites and polymers.

Extracting Metals

- Many of the first metals discovered by humans were low on the reactivity series.
- As they were unreactive it meant that the metals could be found in their pure form, e.g. gold and silver, and were not in a compound.
- Other, more reactive, metals tended to have already reacted with other elements, such as oxygen, to form compounds.
- One of the biggest milestones in human history was stumbling upon the displacement reaction using carbon that can be used to purify iron ore:
  - Iron is heated in a furnace with carbon and limestone
  - Carbon is higher in the reactivity series than iron so displaces the iron
  - Molten iron is formed and the carbon joins on to the oxygen forming carbon dioxide.

> ### Key Point
>
> All metals below carbon in the reactivity series can be extracted using this method.

iron ore, carbon and limestone

waste gases

molten iron flow

liquid waste

carbon + iron oxide $\longrightarrow$ carbon dioxide + iron
$C(s) \ + \ 2FeO(s) \ \longrightarrow \ CO_2(g) \ + 2Fe(l)$

Ceramics

- Ceramics are made from heating non-metallic materials at high temperatures.
- The properties of the ceramic material differ from the initial material, e.g. ceramic pots are very different to the clay used to make them.
- This is because the high temperatures cause crystals to form on cooling.
- By controlling the speed of cooling, different sized crystals can be made.
- Rapid cooling causes small crystals and slow cooling causes large crystals.

- If other minerals are added to glass when it is formed, glass ceramics can be made.
- Although they are often brittle, these can tolerate very high temperatures, so are often used as cookware (e.g. Pyrex) or in laboratories.

Polymers

- It is possible to join small molecules (monomers) together in long chains.
- The chained molecule consisting of repeating monomer units is called a polymer.
- Polymers are extremely useful because they can be used to create different materials, e.g. the monomer ethene can be made into poly(ethene).
- Poly(ethene) is used to make plastic bags and bottles.

ethene   poly(ethene)

n means a large number of, or many

Composites

- A composite is a material that is made from two or more different materials bonded (joined) together.
- The new composite material has different characteristics to those of the starting materials.
- Concrete, first made by the Romans, is made from mixing cement with different stones. The resulting mixture is far stronger than the cement or the stones alone.
- Carbon fibre is a very light and exceptionally strong composite formed from sheets of carbon fibre bonded together with a resin.
- Carbon fibre materials are used when strength is needed with low weight; for example, helicopter rotor blades, airplanes and kayaks.

> **Quick Test**
>
> 1. Why were gold and silver amongst the first elements discovered?
> 2. How would you create small crystals in clay?
> 3. What is a composite?
> 4. Explain how to make a polymer.

> **Key Words**
>
> ceramic
> monomer
> polymer
> composite

Chemistry

Using our Earth Sustainably

You must be able to:

- Describe the structure of the Earth
- Explain rock formation and the rock cycle
- Describe the composition of the Earth and its atmosphere.

The Structure of the Earth

- The Earth is a planet in orbit around the Sun.
- All of the chemicals used in industry come from the Earth.
- Rocks make up the solid crust of the Earth.
- The rocks in the crust contain chemical compounds and elements that can be extracted and used.

The Rock Cycle

- There are three types of rocks, classified according to how they formed.
- **Igneous** rock is formed from cooled magma.
  - If the magma cools rapidly, the igneous rock formed is dense and has small crystals, e.g. granite
  - If the magma cools slowly then the igneous rock will be less dense and have large crystals, e.g. basalt.
- When rocks have been subjected to weathering and erosion, pieces of rock break off.
- The sediments formed eventually settle and are subjected to large pressures from the rock above.
- When material deposited in this way forms rock it is called **sedimentary** rock.
- Any material that can be deposited can lead to sedimentary rock, e.g. eroded rock material, or the calcite skeletons of microorganisms that lived in the sea.
- Due to the movement of the tectonic plates, rock that was on or near the surface can be moved closer to the Earth's core.
- Subjected to intense heat and pressure, the structure of the rock alters.
- The altered rock becomes **metamorphic** rock.

Structure of the Earth

core

crust

mantle

Sedimentary rock

Igneous rock

Metamorphic rock

Composition of the Earth

- The chemicals in the Earth's crust tend to be insoluble compounds. If they were soluble, the ground would dissolve whenever it rained!

Element	Abundance (%)
Oxygen	46
Silicon	28
Aluminium	0.8
Iron	0.5
Other elements	24.7

- The atmosphere of the Earth contains very light compounds that exist as gases, as well as very small solid particles that are light enough to float in the air.

Element	Abundance (%)
Nitrogen	78
Oxygen	21
Argon	0.9
Carbon dioxide	0.04
Other trace gases	0.06

Key Point

The composition of elements is very different in different parts of the Earth. It is important to specify which part you are describing.

Quick Test

1. What are the three types of rock?
2. Why do chemicals in the lithosphere tend to be insoluble?
3. Draw the rock cycle.

Key Words

igneous
sedimentary
metamorphic

Using our Earth Sustainably

You must be able to:

- Describe the carbon cycle
- Explain the impact of human activity on the atmosphere
- Describe what is present in the atmosphere and how it has changed over time
- Suggest why the Earth is a source of limited resources.

The Carbon Cycle

- The element carbon (C) is common on Earth.
- Carbon is reactive and can form up to four bonds with different elements, often forming chains.
- The different reactions that carbon takes part in mean that carbon atoms move through the carbon cycle.
- Changes to parts of the cycle will have an impact on other parts of the cycle.

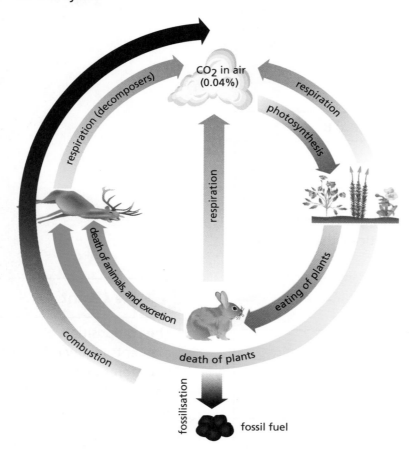

Human Activity and Climate Change

- Human activity can alter the balance in the carbon cycle.
- By removing and burning fossil fuels (coal, oil and natural gas), carbon that was trapped for millions of years is now released into the atmosphere as carbon dioxide.

> **Key Point**
>
> Levels of CO_2 are globally the highest they have been for the past 3 million years.

- This carbon dioxide acts as a greenhouse gas, trapping heat from the Sun.
- The more carbon dioxide released, the hotter the planet becomes – the consequence of this is climate change.
- In different parts of the world, the oceans get warmer.
- This causes changes to currents and wind patterns, and unpredictable and extreme weather patterns can occur.
- Humans produce carbon dioxide through a number of activities:
    - factories or transport (e.g. planes, cars) using fossil fuels
    - cutting down and burning forests.
- Scientific consensus indicates that the amount of carbon dioxide in the atmosphere needs to be reduced.
- Before industrialisation in the 1800s the amount of carbon dioxide in the atmosphere was 0.028%.
- In 2013 the level reached 0.04% for the first time in the past 3 million years.

Limited Resources

- Although the planet looks enormous to us and seems to have an endless supply of resources, this is not true:
    - Many elements that we find most useful are also rare
    - Many of the components used in mobile phones and tablets are made using rare earth metals
    - The majority of the energy we use comes from non-renewable sources, such as coal, oil and natural gas
    - Most items in households of the Western world are made from the products of crude oil.
- The finite reserves of oil are being used up, and since oil takes millions of years to form, we cannot make more. This means that we need to recycle items.
- Recycling involves extracting parts of a used product and making them available for other processes or products, e.g. recycling paper involves collecting the used paper, sorting it and then treating it to make recycled paper.
- Of course, recycling uses energy to extract the materials.
- Manufacturers are increasingly being required by law to make the extraction and recycling of materials easy.

Key Point

Although the media often show both sides of an argument, it is important to recognise when one side has far more scientific evidence than another.

Quick Test

1. What do scientists believe is causing CO_2 levels to increase?
2. What is recycling?
3. Draw the carbon cycle.
4. How are humans affecting the Earth's atmosphere?

Key Words

carbon cycle
fossil fuels
consensus
recycling

Explaining Physical Changes

1 The diagram below shows the arrangement of atoms in four different substances.

A

B

C

D

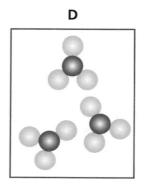

a) Which box has a substance that is a mixture of compounds? [1]

b) Which box has a substance that could be carbon dioxide? [1]

c) Which box has a substance that is a pure element? [1]

2 It is winter and Sylvia has gone to look at her fishpond. The water pump is switched off. There is a layer of ice over the top of the pond. Despite the ice, the fish in the pond are alive and are able to swim.

a) Explain what property, unique to water, has enabled the fish in the pond to survive. [3]

b) Sylvia's sister Hilary suggests breaking the ice and switching the water pump back on.

Explain why this could lead to the death of the fish in the pond. [3]

Explaining Chemical Changes

1 **a)** Write the word equation for the reaction of sodium and chlorine. [2]

b) Write the chemical equation for the reaction of sodium, Na, and chlorine, Cl. [2]

2 Hydrogen peroxide is a chemical that acts as a bleach.

To decompose hydrogen peroxide into water and oxygen the chemical manganese dioxide needs to be present.

a) Write the word equation for the decomposition of hydrogen peroxide. [2]

b) Manganese dioxide is neither a reactant nor a product. What is the chemical name for this type of chemical? [1]

3 In 2012 Feliz Baumgartner floated in a helium balloon until he reached a height of 39 km before jumping out.

a) The diagram below shows a balloon that is floating.

Copy the diagram and draw arrows inside the balloon to represent the pressure of the gas inside and arrows representing the air pressure outside the balloon. [2]

b) Draw the arrangement of particles before and after the air inside the balloon was heated. [1]

Chemistry > Practice Questions

Obtaining Useful Materials

1 The list below is a shortened reactivity series. Use it to answer the following questions.

potassium
sodium
calcium
aluminium
carbon
iron
tin

a) Which of the metals can be extracted from their ores by reacting with carbon? [2]

b) What would be the products of the displacement reaction between carbon and tin carbonate?

Complete the word equation.

carbon + tin carbonate ⟶ .... + ...
[2]

2 What are the small units called that make up a polymer? [1]

3 The volcanic rock basalt is one of the most common rocks on the Earth. It has small crystals that can only be seen clearly using a microscope.

Suggest how quickly basalt cooled and why it would lead to crystals of a small size. [2]

4 Colin is studying the architecture of the Roman Civilisation. He reads that the Romans were the first to make concrete. Concrete is made from stones and cement.

Explain why concrete is a composite material and suggest why the Romans chose to use concrete in their buildings, rather than cement or stones on their own. [2]

Using our Earth Sustainably

1 The Earth consists of layers. Copy the picture below and add labels to identify each layer. [3]

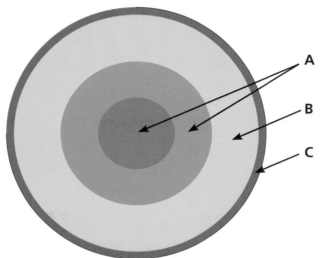

2 The rock cycle below is missing some labels. Copy the diagram and fill in the gaps. [5]

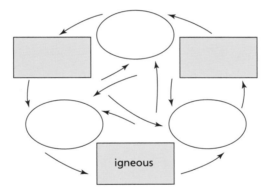

3 The IUPCC has provided evidence that man's activities are a direct cause of climate change.

a) What is climate change? [1]

b) Which of the following are direct causes of climate change?

  i) using nuclear power stations

  ii) manufacturing plastics from crude oil

  iii) geothermal energy

  iv) petrol powered cars [2]

4 Explain why it is important to recycle resources. [2]

Forces and their Effects

You must be able to:

- Describe some causes and effects of forces
- Explain how objects can be affected by forces
- Use force arrows to show forces acting on objects
- Explain the concept of moments
- Describe and explain Hooke's Law.

What are Forces?

- **Forces** are pushes or pulls between two objects.
- Force arrows can be drawn to show the direction that the force is acting in:

- When forces act on an object there will be a consequence:
  - The object can become deformed, e.g. stretched or squashed
  - The object can warm up due to rubbing and the friction between the surfaces
  - The object can be pushed out of the way
  - The object can provide resistance to the motion of water or air.

Balanced and Unbalanced Forces

- Forces act in opposite pairs and force arrows are drawn to show this.
- The forces acting on an object can either be:

Balanced	Unbalanced
This means that there will be no change in the object.	This means that there will be a change in the object.
The upward push of the shelf is balanced by the downward pull of the earth.	The driving force of the cycle is greater than the air resistance - the force is unbalanced. The cyclist is accelerating.

> **Key Point**
>
> You should clearly identify the direction forces act in using arrows.

Measuring Forces

- Forces are measured in Newtons (N).
- The stronger the force, the greater the value in Newtons.
- Forces can be measured using a Newton meter.
- The size of a force can also be measured by the size of the force's effect.
- When an object is stretched or squashed the length can be measured.
- The greater the force applied, the greater the stretch or squashing force.
- There is a linear relationship between the size of the force and the resulting stretch (i.e. they change in proportion to each other).
- This means that for every unit of force, there will be the same effect on the stretch (e.g. 1 N causes 3 cm stretch, 2 N causes 6 cm stretch, 10 N causes 30 cm, etc.)

> **Key Point**
>
> The unit for force, the Newton, must ALWAYS be written with a capital N.

Pivots and Moments

- A pivot is used to turn things.
- A moment is the turning effect of a force, and has the unit Nm.
- moment = force x distance from pivot.

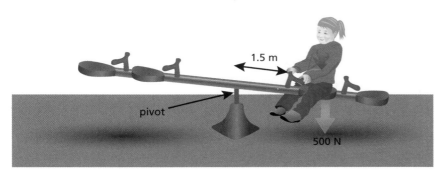

1.5 m

pivot

500 N

- The further away from the pivot, the greater the moment.
- This is why a long-handled screwdriver can be used to open a tin of paint.

Hooke's Law

- Hooke's Law states that the stretch of a spring will be directly proportional to the force applied (i.e. there is a linear relationship between them).

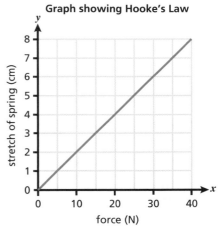

Graph showing Hooke's Law

stretch of spring (cm) vs force (N)

> **Quick Test**
>
> 1. How do we describe a pair of forces if one force is larger than the other? unbalanced
> 2. What is the unit for force? newtons
> 3. What do force arrows tell us? which direction the force
> 4. What is meant by the term moment?
>
> the turning effect of a force
>
> 4/4

> **Key Words**
>
> force
> Newton
> pivot
> moment

Forces and their Effects

You must be able to:

- Explain simple effects of forces on speed and direction
- Calculate speed from distance and time
- Explain how work is done when a force acts on an object and changes it
- Explain how deformation involves work.

Forces and Motion

- An object will move in the direction a force is applied.
- The larger the force, the faster the object will start to move.
- Applying a large enough counter force in the opposite direction to an object's movement will cause the object to slow down and stop, for example, a football net catching a football.

- To change an object's **speed**, a force has to be applied.
- For an object to speed up, more force is needed in the direction of movement.

- For an object to slow down, the force has to be in the opposite direction to the direction of movement.

> **Key Point**
>
> When forces are balanced an object will continue at the same speed. An object that isn't moving has a speed of 0 m/s. If it isn't already moving, it will continue to not move.

Car travelling on tarmac at constant speed 70 mph.

There is greater friction between the gravel and the car tyres.
To travel at 70 mph, more force has to be produced by the engine.

Speed, Distance and Time

- Speed is a measure of the distance that an object travels in a given time.
- speed = distance / time
- The faster the speed, the further the object travels in a set period of time.
- If an athlete ran 100 m in 10 s then:

  speed = 100 m ÷ 10 s

  = 10 m/s

- The magnitude of the change in speed of an object depends on the size and direction of the force that is applied.

Work and Energy Changes

- In science, work is done if a force has acted on an object and there has been a change in that object.
- So, if an object did not move at all, no work will have been done.
- But, if the object moved faster or slowed down, then work will have been done.
- If the object becomes deformed (squashed or stretched) then work will also have been done.
- Work is measured in Newton metres (Nm), or Joules (J).

> **Key Point**
>
> Work is only done if the object changes speed or shape.

Quick Test

1. Give the unit for speed.
2. What is meant by the term 'work'?
3. A car drives 48 km in 40 min. What is its speed?

Key Words

speed
work
Joule

Exploring Contact and Non-Contact Forces

You must be able to:

- Explain non-contact forces between magnets and static electricity
- Explain electrostatic attraction and repulsion
- Describe the effects of gravity across space.

Non-Contact Forces

- A contact force is applied by one object touching another.
- Forces can also act over a distance. These are called non-contact forces, e.g. magnetism, static electricity and gravity.

Magnetism

- Magnets have two poles, North and South.
- The opposite poles of a magnet **attract**.
- The same poles of a magnet **repel**.

Magnets attracting and repelling

repelling   attracting

> ### Key Point
>
> Always remember to write both poles on diagrams of magnets.

Static Electricity

- Static electricity occurs when an object gains or loses electrons (negative charge).
- If the object gains electrons it becomes negative; if it loses electrons it becomes positive.
- If two objects with the same charge are brought together, they will repel each other.
- If an object with a negative charge is brought near an object with positive charge, they will be attracted.

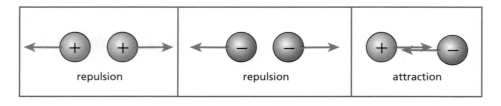

Electric Fields

- When an electric current passes through a wire it produces an **electric field**.
- Electric fields act across the spaces between objects that are not in contact with one another.

Charged parallel plates

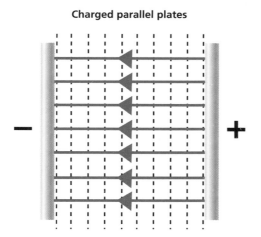

Gravity

- Gravity is a force exerted by one object on another when they are near each other.
- On the Earth everything is pulled to the Earth's centre.
- The Earth has a gravitational field strength of 10 N per kg. This means every kilogram on Earth has a force of 10 N acting on it.
- Every object with mass has a **weight**, measured in N.
- weight = mass x gravitational field strength
- Mass is the measure of all the matter in an object, and has the units kg.
- On other planets and moons the gravitational field strength will be different. The weight of an object will therefore be different on each planet, but the mass will stay the same.
- All objects with mass have a gravitational pull, even people. As the earth is so massive, we do not notice these gravitational pulls.
- The further away you are from the centre of mass causing the gravitational field, the weaker the gravitational force. For example, a person standing on the top of Mount Everest will experience slightly less gravitational pull than a person standing in Trafalgar Square, London.

> **Key Point**
>
> Even in space there is still gravity. When someone is 'weightless' it is because everything is falling at the same time.

> **Key Point**
>
> Gravitational field strength is measured in N/kg.

> **Quick Test**
>
> 1. What is the difference between weight and mass?
> 2. Why does weight decrease with distance from the Earth?
> 3. What forms around a wire when electric current flows through it? ~~Sta~~ electric's ~~ty~~ field
> 4. Draw two magnets repelling and attracting.

> **Key Words**
>
> attract
> repel
> electric field
> weight

Exploring Contact and Non-Contact Forces

You must be able to:

- Explain how pressure acts in the atmosphere, in liquids and in solids
- Explain pressure as the effect of force over area
- Explain why objects float and sink.

Pressure

- Forces can act over an area, in all directions.
- **pressure** = force / area
- Pressure is measured in Newtons per metre squared (N/m²).
- A person wearing snowshoes exerts less pressure on the ground than a person of the same mass wearing ice skates.

> ### Key Point
>
> Make sure that the unit is written N/m² and not Nm, which is the unit for the moment of a force.

Atmospheric Pressure

- The atmosphere on the Earth is exerting a pressure on all objects on the surface.
- As an object gets higher, atmospheric pressure reduces, because there is less atmosphere pushing downwards.

pressure at surface = 101,000 N/m²

Pressure in Liquids

- With liquids, pressure increases with depth.
- The deeper an object gets, the greater the force acting on it due to the weight of the liquid above.
- The pressure at the top of the bottle is less than the pressure towards the bottom. Water pours out of the bottom hole much faster than the hole at the top.

Water coming out of 3 holes in a bottle

Upthrust

- When an object is placed into water, the water exerts a force in the opposite direction to the weight of the object.
- The term for this is **upthrust**.
- The more dissolved salts in the water, the greater the upthrust.
- Many ships have a series of lines, called **plimsoll lines**, painted on the hull to show how deep the ship will sink in different waters. In fresh water a ship will sink lower whilst in very salty water, such as in the Dead Sea, the ship will sink less due to the increased upthrust.

upthrust

water   weight

Floating and Sinking

- An object will float if the upthrust equals the weight of the object.
- If the weight is greater than the upthrust, the object will sink.
- Another important consideration is the **density** of the object. The greater the density, the more likely it will be that the weight will overcome the upthrust from the liquid and the object will sink.
- Ships float even though they may weigh thousands of kg because the weight is spread over a large area.

> ### Key Point
>
> Remember – when the forces acting on an object are balanced it will continue to do what it was doing. If it is floating, it will continue to float.

Upthrust / downthrust of blocks in water

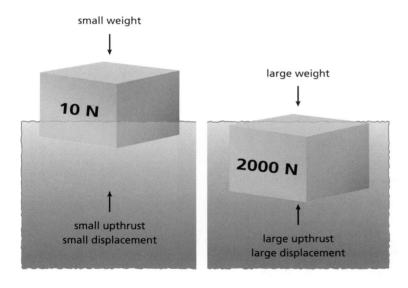

small weight

10 N

small upthrust
small displacement

large weight

2000 N

large upthrust
large displacement

> ### Quick Test
>
> 1. Why does atmospheric pressure decrease with height?
> 2. What is the unit for pressure?
> 3. If an object is floating with weight of 1000 N what is the upthrust?
> 4. For an object to float higher in water, what must be increased?

> ### Key Words
>
> pressure
> upthrust
> plimsoll line
> density

Obtaining Useful Materials

1 Which of the following metals was discovered thousands of years ago? [1]

Gold

Aluminium

Iron

Zinc

2 **a)** Predict which **two** of the following reactions will take place.

    i) copper + aluminium nitrate   **ii)** iron + copper sulfate

    iii) iron + potassium nitrate   **iv)** copper + silver nitrate [2]

    b) For each of the reactions you selected, write the complete word equation for the reaction. [2]

3 The photo shows a blast furnace. A blast furnace is used to extract iron from its ore.

Explain what happens when carbon and iron are reacted together in the blast furnace. [3]

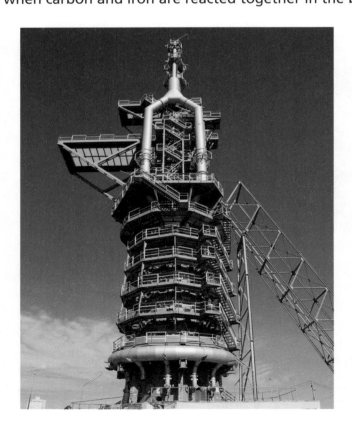

Using our Earth Sustainably

1 Match the rock description to the type of rock:

Rock type	Rock Description
Igneous	has layers of crystals
Sedimentary	has veins, has a waxy appearance and is often used for statues
Metamorphic	is very hard and made of lots of small crystals

[3]

2 Copy the table and use the words below to complete the gaps, showing the abundance of elements in the lithosphere.

aluminium   iron   oxygen   silicon

Element	Abundance (%)
	46
	28
	0.8
	0.5
Other elements	24.7

[4]

3 A group of friends are talking about recycling.

I think that recycling takes up energy so is not worth doing.

Recycling leads to rare materials being extracted and used for other purposes.

There are plenty of resources. This is just an excuse to raise taxes.

We are running out of oil which means we will no longer be able to make plastics.

Kalum   Ruth   Carlos   Arwen

a) Which two friends are giving reasons **for** recyling? [1]

b) Write a counter argument to address Kalum's point. [2]

Forces and their Effects

1 Four Newton meters are shown in the diagram below. Which shows the highest amount of force? [1]

A   B   C D

2 Sandy is playing with balancing scales. On the left-hand scale she has a ball and on the right she adds mass until it balances.

a) If she adds 200 g, what is the mass of the ball in grams? [1]

b) She now removes the ball and puts two blocks on the left-hand scale and 300 g on the right hand scale to balance it. What is the mass of one block in grams? [1]

3 Arran is training to run the 800 m in the Olympics. In her last race she won in 1 min 48 s. What was her average speed for the race? [2]

4 Joss is prising open the lid on a tin of paint. Calculate the **turning moment** for the force applied to the screwdriver.

Show your working and give the correct unit. [3]

force = 15 N

distance = 10 cm

Exploring Contact and Non-Contact Forces

1 Fiesa brings two magnets together. They repel.

a) Copy and complete the diagram to show the poles on the magnets.

Magnet 1   Magnet 2

| | | | | | [2]

b) What would Fiesa have to do to make the magnets attract?   [2]

2 Taking the gravitational field strength on Earth to be 10 N/kg, what would each of the following masses weigh?

    10 kg   15.5 kg   2000 g   [3]

3 The bottle of fizzy drink is full. The bottle has three holes made at points A, B and C.

a) Draw what would happen to the flow of fizzy drink at points A, B and C on the bottle.   [1]

b) Explain why the flow at points A, B and C is different.   [2]

4 Amy and George are both the same weight, 600 N. Amy wears snowshoes with an area of 250 cm² and George wears skis with an area of 350 cm². Calculate the pressure exerted by each of them on the snow.   [2]

Motion on Earth and in Space

You must be able to:

- Interpret distance–time graphs
- Explain and apply concepts of balanced forces and equilibria to analyse stationary objects
- Explain relative motion.

Describing Motion

- The motion of an object (the journey it takes) can be described by drawing a distance–time graph.
- The axes of the graph must be labelled correctly.
- Time is plotted on the *x*-axis.
- Distance is plotted on the *y*-axis.

- The line of a distance–time graph represents the speed the object is travelling at:
  - A steeper line means more distance is covered in the same time, i.e the speed is faster
  - A shallower line means less distance is covered in the same time, i.e. the speed is slower
  - When the line is horizontal it means the object is not moving at all. It has stopped.
- A more complex distance–time graph appears below:

Relative Motion

- The motion of objects is always **relative** to the **observer**.
- If two trains, A and B, are travelling at the same speed on tracks parallel to one another it would appear to an observer on either train that both trains were at a standstill.
- If the trains were travelling on parallel tracks towards each other at the same speed, then an observer on either of the trains would get the impression that the other train was travelling at twice the speed of their train.
- To calculate relative velocity to an observer:
    - If the object is moving towards the observer, add the speeds.
    - If the object is moving away from the observer, subtract the speeds.
- So for trains moving parallel to each other:

    Observer ⟶ 10 m/s
    Object ⟶ 10 m/s

    relative velocity = 10 m/s – 10 m/s = 0 m/s
- For trains moving in opposite directions:

    Observer ⟶ 10 m/s
    Object ⟵ 10 m/s

    relative velocity = 10 m/s + 10 m/s = 20 m/s

Key Point

The position of an observer may influence what they see. Everything is relative!

Key Point

Velocity is the same as speed, but with direction added.

Forces in Equilibrium

- When forces act in opposite directions to each other and are the same size, they are balanced or in **equilibrium**.
- When the forces are balanced, the object will continue to do what it is doing:
    - If it is moving, it will move at a constant speed.
    - If it is stationary, it will stay stationary.
- A spring with a 10 N weight attached will stretch until the force of the spring pulling the weight upwards (the **reaction force**) equals 10 N.

 Quick Test

1. If an apple produces 1 N of force on a desk, it is not moving. What is the reaction force?
2. What can a distance–time graph tell us?
3. One car travels left at 70 mph and another travels right at 60 mph. What is the relative speed?
4. What does the slope tell you on a distance–time graph?

 Key Words

relative
observer
equilibrium
reaction force

Motion on Earth and in Space

You must be able to:

- Explain differences in gravity on different planets
- Explain why the Earth has seasons
- Explain why day length varies on both the Earth's hemispheres.

Space and Gravity

- Gravity is a force that gives objects weight.
- Every object with mass has gravity.
- Gravity, however, is a relatively weak force and a very large mass is needed before the gravitational pull is noticed.
- Therefore, all planets and moons (not just Earth) have a gravitational pull.
- Weight is calculated by the formula:

> **weight = mass x gravitational field strength (*g*)**

- The Earth has a gravitational field strength (*g*) of 10 Newtons per kilogram, which is written as: ***g* = 10 N/kg**
- On other planets and moons the value of *g* will differ.

Planets, showing approximate gravitational field strength values (N/kg)

| Mercury | Venus | Earth | Mars | Jupiter | Saturn | Uranus | Neptune |
| 4 N/kg | 9 N/kg | 10 N/kg | 4 N/kg | 25 N/kg | 11 N/kg | 9 N/kg | 12 N/kg |

- The gravitational field strength of the Earth keeps the Moon in orbit, whilst the much larger gravitational field strength of the Sun keeps the Earth and all the other planets in orbit around it.
- The Sun is our closest star and it orbits the centre of our galaxy, the Milky Way.
- The Milky Way is filled with billions of other stars, all orbiting the galactic centre due to the gravitational pull from a black hole in the centre.
- Our galaxy is only one of billions, all exerting a gravitational pull on each other.
- Distances in space are enormous, so scientists use the astronomical unit for distance, the light year.
- A light year is the distance that light travels in 1 earth year, 9,460,730,472,580,800 km or 9.5 trillion km.

> ### Key Point
>
> Do not confuse mass and weight. Weight is a force and changes depending where you are. Mass always stays the same.

The Earth in Space

- The Earth spins on its axis once every 24 hours.
- The Earth is tilted on its axis, so at different times of the year the Northern and Southern Hemispheres receive different amounts of radiation from the Sun. This leads to seasons.
- Day length varies in the two hemispheres as the planet orbits the Sun.

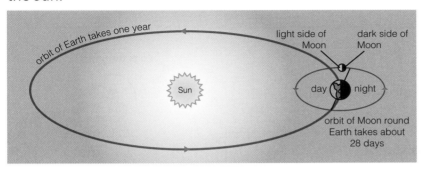

- An **equinox** is when both hemispheres of the Earth receive the same amount of light, so day and night are the same length wherever you are on the planet.
- There are two equinoxes a year, on the 21st March and 21st September.
- Between 21st March and 21st September, days are longer than nights in the Northern Hemisphere. In the Southern Hemisphere the opposite is true.
- After 21st September, day length shortens in the Northern Hemisphere and lengthens in the Southern Hemisphere.
- For the Northern Hemisphere 21st June is the longest day (summer **solstice**) and 21st December the shortest day (winter solstice). This is reversed for those in the Southern Hemisphere.

Northern Hemisphere summer/winter path of sun

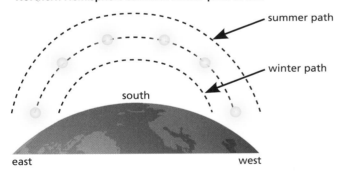

> ## Key Point
>
> If the Earth was not tilted then there would be no seasons. There would be no difference in day length across the planet.

> ## Key Point
>
> The dates given for the equinoxes and solstices are the average. The precise dates vary according to the year.

Quick Test

1. How long does daylight last on 21st March (the spring equinox) in the Northern Hemisphere?
2. Why do we get seasons?
3. If a person weighed 800 N on Earth, what would they weigh on Jupiter, where the gravitational field strength is 25 N/kg?
4. Suggest why *g* is only 4 N/kg on Mercury.

> ## Key Words
>
> gravitational field
>   strength
> light year
> equinox
> solstice

Energy Transfers and Sound

You must be able to:

- Understand and apply the model of energy transfer to various contexts
- Explain the role and significance of fuels.

Energy Changes Due to Forces

- When force is applied, work can be calculated using the formula:

> **work = force x distance**

- Increasing the distance to the pivot means less force is applied, but over a larger distance. Reducing the distance increases the force used. The amount of work always remains the same.
- Similarly, gears increase the distance to the pivot, with a smaller gear turning many times, making a larger gear move.
- When an object changes its motion, other changes are experienced, e.g. dropping an object causes changes in the energy in the object. The energy is transformed from gravitational potential to kinetic energy.

Cogs turning

GPE = 100% KE = 0%	GPE = 50% KE = 50%	GPE = 0% KE = 100%
1 The instant the object leaves the hand all of its energy is in the form of gravitational potential energy.	2 When the object is half-way to the ground, half the energy will be gravitational potential energy and the other half kinetic energy.	3 At the instant the object hits the ground, all of its energy is in the form of kinetic energy.

- A dynamo is a device that converts the movement of a wheel into electrical energy to power a lightbulb or recharge a battery cell by transforming kinetic to electrical energy.
- The more efficient a transfer, the less wasted energy there is.

> ### Key Point
>
> Often some of the energy is 'lost' as heat and sound. We say it is transferred.

Energy Changes Due to Altering Matter

- When forces are applied to an object they will change its shape.
- When compression is applied to a spring, energy is stored as elastic energy.
- When the spring is released, it returns to its original shape.

- The elastic energy is transformed to kinetic energy as it decompresses.
- Fuel has its energy stored in the form of **chemical potential energy**.
- When a source of ignition is provided the energy in the fuel is released through combustion and this happens very quickly:

> **fuel + oxygen ⟶ carbon dioxide + water +** **energy**

- The energy released is heat, but some energy may be transformed into light.
- There are many types of fuels, storing different amounts of chemical potential energy.
- Most of the fuels in current use derive from crude oil although the number of alternatives, such as biodiesel, are increasing.
- The metabolism of food is similar to the combustion of fuel.
- The process inside cells is called respiration. It happens more slowly than combustion and involves food (the fuel) reacting with oxygen:

> **food + oxygen ⟶ carbon dioxide + water + energy**

- When hot and cold objects come together, heat energy will transfer into the cooler object, until both objects are the same temperature.

> **Key Point**
>
> You can't let the cold in, only the heat out!

Energy Changes Due to Vibrations and Waves

- The Sun warms the Earth by radiation.
- Radiation is the transfer of heat energy via waves (infrared) that can travel in a vacuum.
- The objects do not need to be touching to receive the heat energy.
- **Vibration** of atoms occurs when objects get hot.
- The more kinetic energy, the more vibrations there are and the hotter they get.

Energy Changes Due to Electricity

- In an electric circuit the battery stores chemical potential energy.
- When the circuit is completed, the chemical potential energy is transformed into electrical energy – carried by the electric charge that moves around the circuit.

> **Quick Test**
>
> 1. What is the word equation for the combustion of fuel in oxygen?
> 2. Describe the differences in reaction rate between combustion and respiration.
> 3. What is meant by radiation in terms of energy transfers?
> 4. An object has gravitational potential energy of 1000 J. What will its maximum kinetic energy be?

> **Key Words**
>
> gravitational potential energy
> kinetic energy
> compression
> chemical potential energy
> vibration

Energy Transfers and Sound

You must be able to:

- Explain how sound waves behave
- Explain how different animals hear
- Explain how sound is produced.

Sound Waves

- Sound waves carry energy through a medium.
- The medium must have particles to transfer energy as sound.
- The closer the particles, the faster the energy can be transferred.
- Sound travels fastest in solids, slower in liquids and slowest in gases.
- The speed of sound in air is 340 m/s, in water it is 1500 m/s and in solids such as wood, 4000 m/s.
- The **frequency** of a wave is measured in hertz (1 Hz = 1 wave per second).
- Musical notes have separate frequencies.
- Animals can hear a range of sounds.
- As humans get older, the range of hearing decreases, with the highest frequency sounds being lost first.
- Objects produce sound when they vibrate. For example:
  1. A guitar string when plucked causes a vibration in the wire.
  2. The wire hits air particles and causes them to move.
  3. The air particles collide with other air particles. Eventually they make the ear drum vibrate at the same frequency.
- Loudspeakers work in a similar way:
  1. Music is converted to an electrical signal which causes electromagnets to move a fabric skin or membrane.
  2. The fabric skin's motion causes air particles to move.
  3. Eventually the sound waves reach the ear.
- Microphones work in the opposite way:
  - Sound waves produced by an instrument or voice hit a membrane attached to magnets
  - The motion of the magnets causes a changing electrical signal that can be recorded and used to make a loudspeaker move.

> **Key Point**
>
> A vacuum does not contain particles, so sound cannot travel in a vacuum.

Hearing range of animals

Sound from loudspeaker

Using Sound

- Very high frequency sound (greater than 20000 Hz) can be used to clean objects, e.g. jewellers can clean jewellery using an ultrasonic bath. The high frequency vibrations cause minute particles of dirt to be displaced.
- **Ultrasound** is also used in medicine, e.g. to treat injuries and to detect the movement of a developing foetus in the mother's uterus.

Echoes and Absorption

- Sound waves behave like any other wave, which means that they can be reflected:

reflecting surface

- When sound waves reflect straight back an **echo** is heard.
- When echoes would be a problem, e.g. in a music recording studio, steps are taken to prevent any echoes from spoiling the recording.
- Putting special angled tiles onto the walls and ceilings ensures that the sound waves keep reflecting within the tile until the energy has been **absorbed**.

> **Key Point**
>
> For an echo to be heard, the sound must reflect off an object. The smoother the object, the better.

Quick Test

1. What does it mean if a wave has a frequency of 50 Hz?
2. Explain how echoes occur.
3. Suggest how to reduce echoes in a sound studio.
4. Explain how a loudspeaker works.

Key Words

frequency
ultrasound
echo
absorb

Forces and their Effects

1 Look at the following diagrams showing an astronaut in space. For (a), (b), and (c), decide whether the astronaut will move or not. [3]

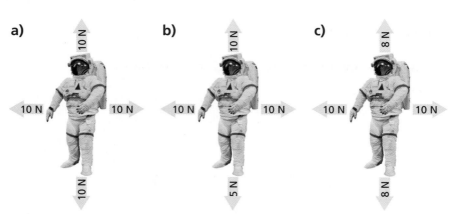

a) 10 N 10 N 10 N 10 N

b) 10 N 10 N 10 N 5 N

c) 8 N 10 N 10 N 8 N

2 Ges is investigating whether a spring obeys Hooke's Law. He hangs masses from a spring and measures the length the spring stretches each time. The table below shows the results for Ges's experiment.

Mass (g)	Weight (N)	Stretch (cm)
0	0	0
100	1	2
200	2	4
300	3	6
400	4	8
500	5	10
600	6	
700	7	
800	8	16

Ges did not record a result for 600 g and 700 g. Predict what the stretch of the spring should have been (in cm) for these. [2]

3 The International Space Station (ISS) orbits the Earth at an average speed of 27,600 km/h.

Taking the distance of one orbit of the Earth as 42,927 km, how long does it take the ISS to orbit the Earth once? Show your working out. [3]

Exploring Contact and Non-Contact Forces

1 Which of the following forces are examples of non-contact forces?

    a) a tug of war   **b)** mass

    c) weight   **d)** static electricity   [2]

2 Charlotte rubs a polythene rod with a cloth and holds it close to a stream of flowing water from the tap.

Normal flow   Flow changes with
of water   a charged rod

    a) Suggest why the water is attracted to the polythene rod.   [2]

    b) Charlotte hangs the charged rod by a piece of string and then brings another rod with the same charge close to it. What will happen to the hanging rod?   [1]

3 A heavy lifting ship sinks below sea level so that it can pick up large objects such as oil rigs. When it sinks, ballast tanks fill with water. The heavy lifting ship does not sink to the bottom of the sea.

Explain, using the photo, why the ship does not sink.   [3]

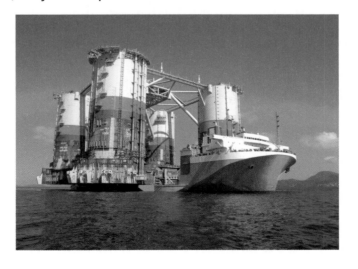

Motion on Earth and in Space

1. Lisa is walking her dog. The distance–time graph below shows Lisa's journey.

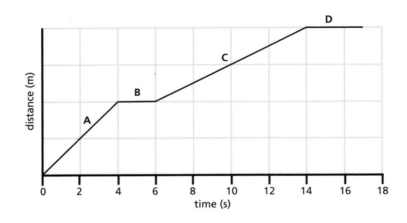

Each of the following describes part of Lisa's journey. Choose which of the labels A–D match with the parts of Lisa's journey given below:

Lisa stopped for 2 min   **Lisa walked for 8 min**

Lisa jogged for 4 min   **Lisa stopped for 3 min**   [4]

2. Two cars are involved in a head-on collision. Luckily the occupants of both cars were not injured.

   If both cars were travelling at 40 km/h, what would the relative speed have been?   [1]

3. The closest star to Earth outside the solar system is Proxima Centauri, which is 4.2 light years from the Earth.

   a) What is a light year?   [1]

   b) Taking the speed of light to be 300,000 km/s in a vacuum, calculate how far away Proxima Centauri is from the Earth in km. Show your working.   [3]

4. The diagram below shows the path the Sun takes in the Northern Hemisphere in June.

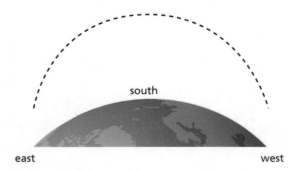

   Copy the diagram and add the path that the Sun will take in December.   [2]

Energy Transfers and Sound

1 A bungee jumper jumps off of a bridge.

 a) At what point does the bungee jumper have the most kinetic energy? [1]

 b) At what point does the bungee jumper have the most gravitational potential energy? [1]

2 The equation below is the word equation for the combustion of a fuel burned in excess oxygen.

> **Fuel + A ⟶ B + C +** ~~energy~~

 a) What are A, B and C? [2]

 b) What is the name of the process in cells that is equivalent to combustion? [1]

3 Which of the following is the way that the Sun heats the Earth?

 a) conduction

 b) convection

 c) radiation

 d) nuclear [1]

4 Jamie is talking to his wife Linda. He is standing in the kitchen and Linda is in the next room.

 Explain why Jamie and Linda can hear each other talking, even though they are not in the same room. [2]

Magnetism and Electricity

You must be able to:

- Explain electric current as a flow of charge
- Apply concepts of potential difference and resistance
- Describe and measure current in series and parallel circuits
- Use formulae to calculate resistance, current, voltage and energy used.

Electric Current

- In an electric circuit, charged electrons move through the wire and components.
- The rate of the flow of charge is called the electric current (I).
- Current is measured in amperes (A) using an ammeter.
- The battery in a circuit provides energy to the charged electrons passing through.
- The battery cell has a negative and positive terminal.
- The potential difference (p.d.) is the work done to move a unit of charge from one point to another in a circuit.
- In an electric circuit diagram the wires and components are drawn in a simple way to show the connections and components.
- A series circuit has a single loop:

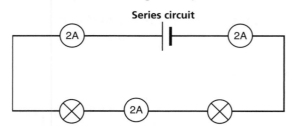

Series circuit

- In parallel circuits the flow of electric current is split between different branches. When the branches meet up, the currents add together again.

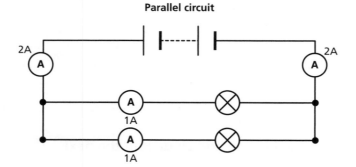

Parallel circuit

- Electricity in the home is connected as a parallel circuit, called a ring main.

> **Key Point**
>
> Potential difference is also known as voltage.

Ammeter

Bulb

Battery

Components and Resistance

- All components in a circuit resist the flow of electric current; they have a **resistance**.
- An electrical **insulator** has complete resistance, allowing no current to flow through. A **conductor** has low resistance to the flow of current.
- Some components are engineered to be electrical insulators under certain conditions and conductors in others, e.g. light dependent resistors.
- Resistance is measured in ohms (Ω).
- The higher the resistance, the slower the flow of electric current through the component, and the energy carried by the charged electrons has time to transfer to the component.
- A light bulb has a resistance, so electric charge can pass energy to the filament of the bulb, which produces light as it heats up.

Key Point

Resistance is the ratio of the p.d. to the current.

Electricity Calculations

- Resistance (R) can be calculated using the following formula:

$$R = V / I$$

- Where R = resistance (Ω), V = potential difference (V) and I = current (A).
- The current in a series circuit is the same all the way around the circuit.
- Electric power (P) is measured in watts (W) and is calculated using the formula:

$$P = V \times I$$

- Amount of energy transferred is calculated using the formula:

$$\textbf{energy transferred (kWh)} = \textbf{power (kW)} \times \textbf{time (h)}$$

Key Point

Kilowatts (kW, 1000 W) are used rather than watts because otherwise the numbers involved get large and difficult to handle very quickly.

Power Ratings

- All electrical equipment has a power rating (in W or kW) which enables you to work out how much they use. The higher the power rating, the more electricity used.
- The time the equipment is switched on for is also important.
- A 2 kW heater switched on for 4 hours uses 2 kW x 4 h = 8 kWh
- Electricity bills charge for electricity based on how many kWh of electricity have been used.

Key Words

series
parallel
resistance
insulator
conductor

Quick Test

1. What is the resistance if the p.d is 1.5 V and the current 3 A?
2. What is the unit for resistance?
3. Explain what an insulator is.
4. Draw a series and parallel circuit, each with 2 bulbs.

Magnetism and Electricity

You must be able to:

- Describe magnetic attraction, repulsion and fields
- Explain the Earth's magnetic field and how it can be used for navigation
- Describe how electromagnets work.

Magnets

- Permanent magnets are made from magnetic metals and alloys.
- The three magnetic metals are iron, cobalt and nickel.
- Magnets have a North and South-seeking pole at each end.
- When two magnets are brought near one another they will either attract or repel each other.

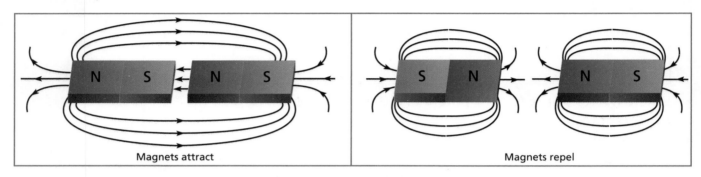

Magnets attract   Magnets repel

- The magnetic field of a magnet is invisible but can be shown using plotting compasses or iron filings sprinkled onto paper.
- The magnetic field can be represented by drawing field lines.

The Earth as a Magnet

- The Earth behaves like a bar magnet because it has a core made of iron and nickel.

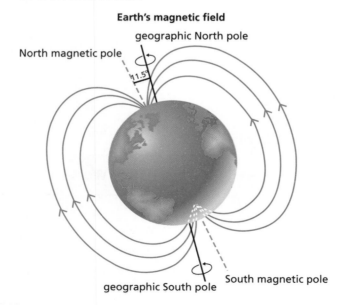

Earth's magnetic field

geographic North pole

North magnetic pole

11.5°

geographic South pole   South magnetic pole

- The poles of the Earth are the equivalent of the poles of a bar magnet.
- Navigation is possible using a handheld compass, which seeks magnetic North.

Electromagnetism

- When an electric current is passed through a wire, it causes a weak magnetic field to be formed.
- The strength of the magnetic field can be increased by:
  - coiling the wire
  - increasing the current flowing through the circuit
  - adding a core made from a magnetic metal, e.g. iron.
- As the magnetic field is temporary and created by an electric current, the magnet formed is called an electromagnet.
- Electromagnets are stronger than permanent magnets and can be turned off.

Magnetic fields through an electric coil

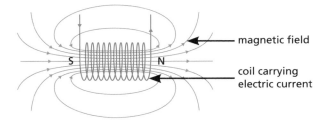

magnetic field

coil carrying
electric current

Uses of Electromagnets

- Electromagnets are used in a number of different ways, e.g. heavy lifting in car breakers yards.
- In a **DC motor**, the wire and core can move freely.
- Brushes enable the wires to make contact without tangling.
- The motor will continue to turn for as long as there is a current.

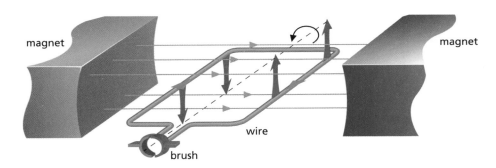

magnet

magnet

wire

brush

> **Quick Test**
>
> 1. Name the ways an electromagnet's strength could be increased.
> 2. Suggest how the Earth's magnetic field is like a bar magnet.
> 3. What does it mean if the magnetic field lines are close together?
> 4. What are the three magnetic metals?

> **Key Words**
>
> magnetic field
> field lines
> electromagnet
> DC motor

Waves and Energy Transfer

You must be able to:

- Explain how waves can be visualised using a ripple tank
- Explain how waves interact to produce interference
- Compare and contrast waves in sound and water with light waves.

Observing Waves

- It is possible to see the shapes of waves as they travel through water.
- The energy causes undulations which travel through the water.
- A ripple tank can be used to view the waves formed when a bar rapidly hits the water.
- When viewed from above the waves can be seen travelling with a transverse motion (at right angles to the direction of travel).
- The waves in water can also be reflected.

> **Key Point**
>
> Remember, the number of waves a second is the frequency. The more often waves appear, the higher the frequency.

Ripple tank with waves

illumination

power supply

oscillating paddle

shallow tank of water

wave patterns on a viewing screen or table

- A wave viewed from the side has the following features:
  - The height of the wave is the amplitude
  - The top of the wave is the peak
  - The distance between a point on one wave and the same point on the next wave is the wavelength.

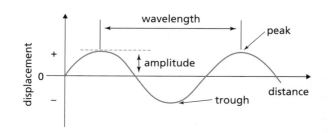

wavelength

peak

amplitude

displacement

trough

distance

- Although the wave moves from left to right, a boat would move up and then down over the same spot.

Boat rotation on a wave

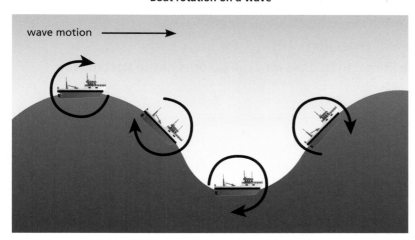

wave motion ⟶

Superposition

- Waves can interact with each other. This is called interference.
- If the peaks and troughs arrive at exactly the same time as the other wave then they will combine to produce waves that are the sum of each contributing wave.
- If the waves arrive out of phase, then they will cancel each other out.

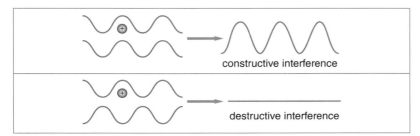

constructive interference

destructive interference

Comparing Sound with Light

- Light travels in waves, but unlike sound or water waves, light does not need a medium (made of particles) to travel through.
- Light can travel in a vacuum (the absence of particles).
- The speed of light in a vacuum is 300,000 km/s.
- In other substances, such as air, water and plastic, the speed of light is slower.

> **Quick Test**
>
> 1. What makes light waves different to sound or water waves?
> 2. What device can be used to look at waves in water?
> 3. Approximately how many times faster does light travel than the speed of sound in air?
> 4. What happens when two waves arrive in phase?

> **Key Words**
>
> transverse
> amplitude
> peak
> interference

Waves and Energy Transfer

You must be able to:

- Explain how light is scattered and reflected off surfaces
- Understand the law of reflection
- Explain how white light can be split into the colours of the spectrum.

Light and Materials

- When light waves hit an object the light may be absorbed or reflected by the object.

Diffuse scattering and specular reflection	
If the surface of the object is rough then the light will be scattered diffusely in a variety of different directions.	If the surface is smooth enough, then the light waves hitting the surface will all bounce off at the same angle.

Reflection

- Light waves can be drawn as rays.
- Light follows the law of **reflection**, which states that

  the angle of incidence = the angle of reflection

- An observer looking at the reflected rays will see an image.

> **Key Point**
>
> Incident and reflected rays are compared to what a normal ray of light would do. A normal is drawn at right angles to the surface.

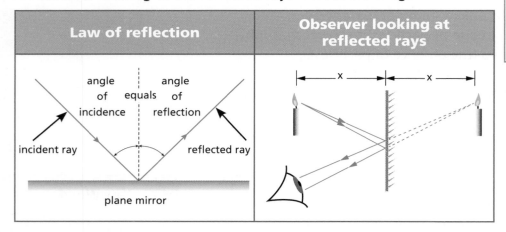

Law of reflection	Observer looking at reflected rays
plane mirror	

The Eye

- The most simple camera is called a pinhole camera.
- It has no lens, just a small hole for light to pass through.

- The eye acts like a pinhole camera.
- The image forms on the retina at the back of the eye. The image information is sent to the brain and the image reversed, so that it is 'seen' the right way up.

Eye as a pinhole camera

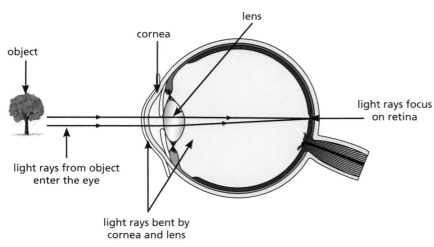

- A **convex** lens brings the light to a focus on the retina by a process called **refraction**.
- Refraction is where light slows as it passes through an optically dense medium or speeds up going into an optically less dense medium.
- Refraction causes the ray to bend.

Seeing Colour

- Light waves carry energy.
- Specialised cells in the eye are hit by the light ray, causing a chemical reaction. An electrical signal is then sent to the brain.
- With a camera the light hits a sensor which then sends an electrical signal to the memory card.
- Visible light is made up of waves of different frequencies.
- A prism splits white light into the colours of the spectrum, based on their **frequency**.
- Objects absorb different frequencies of light.
- The light that is not absorbed is reflected, giving the object colour.

Focus of light on the retina

Key Point

Although we can see millions of different colours, our eyes only have receptors for red, green and blue.

Quick Test

1. What colour is most refracted in white light?
2. What device can split white light into colours?
3. How does a pinhole camera work?
4. What is diffuse scattering?

Key Words

reflection
convex
refraction
frequency

Motion On Earth and in Space

1   Which of the following cars has balanced forces acting on it?

   a)   accelerating to 80 km/h

   b)   deccelerating to 20 km/h

   c)   braking to avoid an accident

   d)   travelling at 60 km/h   [1]

2   The diagram below shows the planets in our solar system.

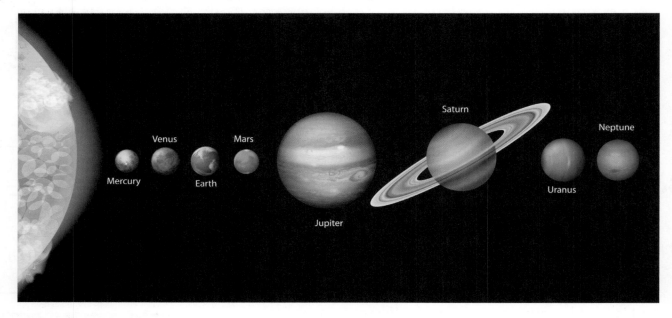

   a)   The planets all orbit the Sun.

      What force keeps the planets in orbit?   [1]

   b)   It takes light 4.1 h to travel from the Sun to Neptune.

      Taking the speed of light to be 300,000 km/s, calculate the distance (in km) of Neptune
      from the Sun.

      Show your working out.   [3]

3   Explain why planet Earth has seasons.   [3]

Energy Transfers and Sound

1 An elephant is being lifted using a lever.

a) Ollie is trying to work out the best way to lift the elephant with the lever. Which of the following suggestions would enable him to lift the elephant more easily?

  i) move the elephant further from the pivot

  ii) use less force

  iii) move the pivot closer to the elephant

  iv) use more force [2]

b) When the elephant is lifted it gains energy. Which of the following types of energy will the elephant have after being lifted?

  i) sound   **ii)** mass   **iii)** kinetic   **iv)** gravitational potential [1]

2 In the UK an anti-loitering device was created to deter teenagers from hanging around shops in large groups. It emitted an extremely loud and annoying high pitched sound.

a) Suggest why teenagers could hear the anti-loitering device and why adults could not. [2]

b) The alarm used a loudspeaker that could vibrate at very high frequencies.
Explain how the sound travelled from the loudspeaker to a teenager's ear. [4]

3 Radar is a system that uses electromagnetic radiation (e.g. microwaves) to reflect off objects. Radar is used to detect airplanes. The USAF Stealth bomber is an airplane that does not reflect electromagnetic radiation.

Which of the following is the best explanation of why the Stealth bomber is invisible to radar.

a) The bomber reflects the radar signal the wrong way.

b) The bomber absorbs the radar signal.

c) The bomber is a good reflector of electromagnetic radiation.

d) The radar travels through the bomber, so there are no reflections. [1]

Magnetism and Electricity

1 Draw a bar magnet, showing the magnetic field lines. [2]

2 Andy and Catherine are building a simple electromagnet.

a) They want to increase the strength of the electromagnet. Which of the following would be ways to increase strength?

i) more turns in the wire

ii) use copper wire

iii) use thicker wire

iv) add an iron core

v) add a plastic core

vi) increase the current [3]

b) Catherine wants to know why an electromagnet can be more useful than a permanent magnet. What should Andy tell Catherine? [1]

3 The parallel circuit below shows four ammeters. If the first ammeter (A1) reads 4 A, what would each of the other ammeters read? [2]

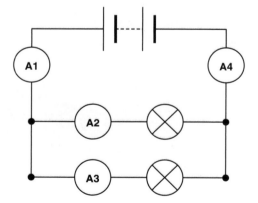

4 a) What current will flow through a 60 W bulb with a voltage of 230 V? [1]

b) Calculate the energy (in kWh) transferred if the bulb was on for 200 hours.

Show your working out. [3]

Waves and Energy Transfer

1 Naveen shines a laser at a mirror. She angles the laser so that it is at 30° to the normal.

Copy the diagram below and add the incident and reflected rays. [3]

2 a) Copy the diagram below and add the labels **peak**, **trough** and **amplitude** to the waves shown. [3]

b) In the diagram, 1 second has passed. What will the **frequency** of the wave be?

Give the correct unit. [2]

3 White light is shone through a prism. What is the order of colours that appear on the screen? [4]

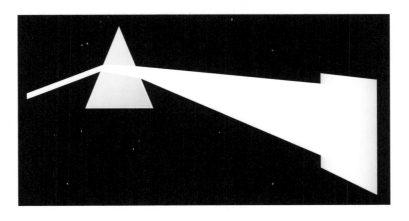

Magnetism and Electricity

1 Which of the following elements are magnetic?

    a) sulfur   **b)** carbon   **c)** cobalt   **d)** vanadium   [1]

2 Which of the following circuits will work?   [1]

 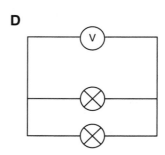

3 The diagram below shows a relay switch. It enables a small, safe circuit to be switched on and, in doing so, turn on a more dangerous circuit with much higher voltages.

    a) What will happen to the electromagnet when the switch is closed?   [1]

    b) Explain what will happen to the armature once the switch is closed.   [2]

Waves and Energy Transfer

1 Explain why we can see our reflection in a mirror but not in a sheet of paper. [3]

2 Roger is using a ripple tank. He sets up the waves with a frequency of 10 Hz.

movement of waves

    a) What does 10 Hz mean? [1]

    b) Copy the picture and add four more waves on the ripple tank. [2]

    c) Roger puts a barrier into the water at an angle.

        On your diagram, draw the reflected waves. [2]

3 Sara is looking at a tree.

    a) Draw the light rays from the top and bottom of the tree and show their route through the eye. [3]

    b) What is the name of the process by which light is bent by the lens? [1]

1 Quetzal is carrying out the distillation of alcohol. He sets up the apparatus as shown in the diagram below.

a) i) On the diagram above, write the letter B where the temperature will be the **highest** in the experiment.

1 mark

ii) On the diagram above, identify the distillate using the letter X.

1 mark

b) Suggest where cold water enters into the distillation tube and why it is important that the cold water flows in at that point.

....

....

....

....

....

2 marks

c) Ethanol is an alcohol.

It has the chemical formula C_2H_6O

How many **atoms** are present in a molecule of ethanol?

Tick the correct box.

2 ☐   8 ☐

3 ☐   9 ☐

☐

1 mark

d) There are a number of state changes that take place during distillation.

In the boxes below draw the particle arrangement for the particles at point Y and at point Z.

☐

1 mark

Point Y   Point Z

TOTAL

☐

6

2 A group of performers are carrying out acrobatics for a TV talent show.

Michael and Kerrie lift a pole from each end and keep it level.

a) If Kerrie has to use 20 N of force to keep her end of the pole up, how much will Michael use to keep it level?

Tick the correct box.

80 N ☐

100 N ☐

20 N ☐

150 N ☐

☐

1 mark

b) Amy vaults onto the middle of the pole and does a handstand.

Amy weighs 600 N.

How much force will Michael have to use to keep balancing the pole with Kerrie?

Show your working out.

....

....

☐

2 marks

c) Nicola is wearing a pair of stilts.

Nicola has a weight of 650 N.

The end of each stilt has an area of 9 cm².

i) What **pressure** would the stilts exert on the ground? Give your answer in N/m².

Show your working out.

2 marks

ii) Describe what Nicola would need to do to exert **less** pressure on the ground.

1 mark

TOTAL

6

3 The lungs are where our body takes in oxygen from the air.

a) The diagram is a model that shows how the human lungs work.

Refer to the model to explain how it shows **breathing in** and **breathing out**.

Breathing in _____

_____

_____

_____

3 marks

Breathing out _____

_____

_____

_____

3 marks

glass tube

glass jar

rubber tubes

balloons

rubber sheet

b) The diagram shows the inside of three breathing airways.

One is **normal**, one is of a **heavy smoker**, and one is of someone with **asthma**.

Complete the label for each diagram.

Choose from these words: **normal**   **smoker**   **asthma**

i) _____   **ii)** _____   **iii)** _____

3 marks

c) Oxygen moves from the lungs to the blood stream by diffusion.

The diagram shows the relative concentrations of oxygen in three different cells.

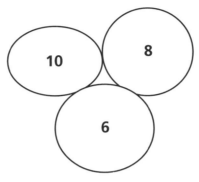

i) Draw three arrows (➜) on the diagram to show the movement of glucose between the three different cells.

3 marks

ii) Explain why oxygen moves between cells in this way.

....

....

3 marks

d) Oxygen is used by the body during aerobic respiration.

There are two types of respiration in humans; aerobic and anaerobic.

i) Other than the use of oxygen, describe two differences between aerobic and anaerobic respiration in humans.

....

....

....

2 marks

ii) Describe the difference between anaerobic respiration in humans and anaerobic respiration in yeast.

....

....

2 marks

TOTAL

19

4 Naveen is investigating how iron reacts with different chemicals.

In her first experiment she added an iron nail to different treatments to see what conditions are needed for rusting to take place.

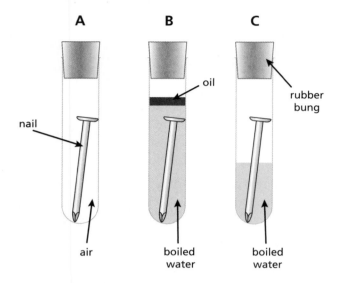

After a week she observed what had happened:

a) In one of the tubes a chemical reaction has taken place.

What evidence is there that a chemical change has taken place?

_____

1 mark

b) Write the **word equation** for the rusting of iron.

_____ + _____ + _____ ⟶ _____

2 marks

c) Suggest what Naveen's **hypothesis** would have been for this experiment.

....

....

....

2 marks

d) Iron is more reactive than copper.

Naveen placed an iron nail into a test tube containing blue copper sulfate solution.

iron nail

blue copper
sulfate solution

i) Suggest what Naveen would **see** in this reaction.

....

....

....

2 marks

ii) Explain your answer.

....

....

....

2 marks

TOTAL

9

5 This question is about plants and animals.

a) Look at the diagram of a food web.

A farmer uses a pesticide to kill leaf-eating insects.

Suggest what effect a reduction of leaf-eating insects would have on the numbers of **blue tits** and **moths**. Explain your answer.

Blue tits ....

....

2 marks

Moths ....

....

2 marks

b) Both plants and animals can respire, but only plants can photosynthesise.

Read the statements about photosynthesis and respiration. Some are true. Some are false.

Put a tick (✓) in the boxes next to the true statements.
Put a cross (✗) in the boxes next to the false statements.

	✓ or ✗
Respiration stores energy as light	
Photosynthesis uses energy from light	
Respiration breaks down large molecules to smaller molecules	
Photosynthesis creates organic molecules from inorganic molecules	
Respiration releases energy from chlorophyll	
Photosynthesis stores energy as light	

6 marks

c) Many species of plants and animals are in danger of extinction.

   i) Red kites are a type of bird found in England. Some people say that red kites were once extinct in England.

   Explain why this is the wrong use of the word extinction.

   ....

   ....

   1 mark

   ii) Dinosaurs once existed. Now they are extinct.

   Suggest what must happen to cause species such as dinosaurs to become extinct.

   ....

   ....

   2 marks

d) Animals and plants are interdependent.

   Complete the diagram to show how animals and plants depend upon one another for **oxygen** and **carbon dioxide**. Write the name of each gas in the correct space.

   plants

   animals

   1 mark

e) Many scientists are responsible for our understanding of the interdependence of plants and animals.

   Which of these statements best describe how scientists work?

   Put ticks (✓) in the boxes next to the **three** best answers.

Most scientific discoveries are the result of a scientist building on the work of a previous scientist	
Once a scientist has an idea they never change their mind	
Scientists never share their ideas with others	
Scientists have their results checked by other scientists	
Scientists use data from experiments to check their ideas	
Scientists never consider risk when doing experiments	

   3 marks

   TOTAL

   17

6 The diagram below shows Katie's toy train.

The pieces are made of wood, but have a magnet at each end.

a) The magnet on carriage X **repelled** the magnet on carriage Y.

The magnet on carriage Y **attracted** the magnet on carriage Z.

i) **On the diagram above**, label the North and South poles of the magnets on X and Z.

1 mark

ii) Katie turned carriage Y around.

The carriage X and carriage Z were **not** turned around.

Describe what would happen now when Katie pushed the parts of the train together.

Explain your answer.

....

....

....

2 marks

b) Katie's brother, Robert, has some metal rods made of different metals.

He takes one of the train carriages and brings each rod close to the magnet on the carriage and observes what happens.

He records his observations in a table.

Complete Robert's table to show what metal (aluminium, magnet or steel) the rods were made of.

Rod	Observation	Metal
A	Attracts whichever side is pointing at the train carriage	
B	Attracts when in one position and repels in the opposite position	
C	Nothing happened	

2 marks

c) Which of the following are magnetic elements?

Tick the correct box(es).

Cobalt ☐

Steel ☐

Iron ☐

Vanadium ☐

1 mark

TOTAL

6

Periodic Table

Key

| relative atomic mass |
| **atomic symbol** |
| name |
| atomic (proton) number |

| 1 |
| **H** |
| hydrogen |
| 1 |

Group 1	Group 2											Group 3	Group 4	Group 5	Group 6	Group 7	Group 0
																	4 **He** helium 2
7 **Li** lithium 3	9 **Be** beryllium 4											11 **B** boron 5	12 **C** carbon 6	14 **N** nitrogen 7	16 **O** oxygen 8	19 **F** fluorine 9	20 **Ne** neon 10
23 **Na** sodium 11	24 **Mg** magnesium 12											27 **Al** aluminium 13	28 **Si** silicon 14	31 **P** phosphorus 15	32 **S** sulfur 16	35.5 **Cl** chlorine 17	40 **Ar** argon 18
39 **K** potassium 19	40 **Ca** calcium 20	45 **Sc** scandium 21	48 **Ti** titanium 22	51 **V** vanadium 23	52 **Cr** chromium 24	55 **Mn** manganese 25	56 **Fe** iron 26	59 **Co** cobalt 27	59 **Ni** nickel 28	63.5 **Cu** copper 29	65 **Zn** zinc 30	70 **Ga** gallium 31	73 **Ge** germanium 32	75 **As** arsenic 33	79 **Se** selenium 34	80 **Br** bromine 35	84 **Kr** krypton 36
85 **Rb** rubidium 37	88 **Sr** strontium 38	89 **Y** yttrium 39	91 **Zr** zirconium 40	93 **Nb** niobium 41	96 **Mo** molybdenum 42	[98] **Tc** technetium 43	101 **Ru** ruthenium 44	103 **Rh** rhodium 45	106 **Pd** palladium 46	108 **Ag** silver 47	112 **Cd** cadmium 48	115 **In** indium 49	119 **Sn** tin 50	122 **Sb** antimony 51	128 **Te** tellurium 52	127 **I** iodine 53	131 **Xe** xenon 54
133 **Cs** caesium 55	137 **Ba** barium 56	139 **La*** lanthanum 57	178 **Hf** hafnium 72	181 **Ta** tantalum 73	184 **W** tungsten 74	186 **Re** rhenium 75	190 **Os** osmium 76	192 **Ir** iridium 77	195 **Pt** platinum 78	197 **Au** gold 79	201 **Hg** mercury 80	204 **Tl** thallium 81	207 **Pb** lead 82	209 **Bi** bismuth 83	[209] **Po** polonium 84	[210] **At** astatine 85	[222] **Rn** radon 86
[223] **Fr** francium 87	[226] **Ra** radium 88	[227] **Ac*** actinium 89	[261] **Rf** rutherfordium 104	[262] **Db** dubnium 105	[266] **Sg** seaborgium 106	[264] **Bh** bohrium 107	[277] **Hs** hassium 108	[268] **Mt** meitnerium 109	[271] **Ds** darmstadtium 110	[272] **Rg** roentgenium 111							

Elements with atomic numbers 112–116 have been reported but not fully authenticated

*The Lanthanides (atomic numbers 58–71) and the Actinides (atomic numbers 90–103) have been omitted.

Cu and **Cl** have not been rounded to the nearest whole number.

Answers

Page 5 Quick Test
1. cell wall, vacuole, or chloroplast
2. mitochondria
3. diffusion
4. cell, tissue, organ, system, organism

Page 7 Quick Test
1. sperm and egg
2. day 14
3. Insect pollinated — flower is brightly coloured, produces less pollen, produces nectar to attract insects. Accept reverse argument for wind pollinated flower.
4. animal, wind or self-dispersal

Page 9 Quick Test
1. The ribs move up and outward while diaphragm moves downwards.
2. volume decreases, pressure increases
3. diffusion
4. Smoking stops the mechanism for getting rid of mucus. Mucus builds up and causes coughing. Lung infections are more likely and there is a long term risk of cancer.

Page 11 Quick Test
1. Protein, fat, carbohydrate, vitamins, minerals, fibre, water.
2. Obesity, starvation, Kwashiorkor, vitamin deficiency, mineral deficiency, e.g. anaemia, vitamin deficiency, e.g. scurvy.
3. Mouth, oesophagus, stomach, small intestine, large intestine, rectum, anus.
4. Plants make their own food (photosynthesis), animals consume food.

Page 12
1. a) nutrition; growth; reproduction [3]

> MRS GREN - This mnemonic can help you remember the characteristics of living things (Movement, Respiration, Sensitivity, Growth, Reproduction, Excretion, Nutrition).

2. b) i) J on shoulder, elbow, hip or knee [1]
   ii) P on skull or ribs [1]

Page 13
2. a) i; b) ii; c) iii; d) ii; e) ii or iii [5]

> One material may have several different properties.

3. a) iii [1];
   b) i; iii [1 mark for both correct]
   c) the Earth orbits the Sun – 365 days; the Earth rotates once – 1 day; the Moon orbits the Earth – 28 days [3]

> Draw straight lines using a ruler.

Page 14
1.

Membrane	Controls what enters and leaves a cell
Cytoplasm	Where chemical reactions take place
Nucleus	Stores information and controls the cell
Mitochondria	Releases energy from glucose
Cell wall	Supports the cell
Vacuole	Inflates the cell
Chloroplast	Changes light energy into food energy

[1 mark each up to a maximum of 7 marks]

> Draw straight lines using a ruler.

2.

cell wall → nucleus, chloroplast, vacuole, cell membrane, cytoplasm, mitochondria

[1 mark for each label, up to a maximum of 6 marks]

3. iii [1]

Page 15
1. a) A diet that contains the right balance [1] and right amounts [1] of all the nutrients needed.
   b) Three of the following:
   eating too much – obesity
   eating too little – starvation
   not eating enough protein – kwashiorkor
   not eating enough vitamins – lack of different vitamins causes different diseases. Lack of vitamin C causes scurvy.
   not eating enough minerals – lack of iron causes anaemia. Lack of calcium causes soft bones. **[3 marks. 1 for each example and explanation]**

> There is 1 mark for each example with explanation.

2. a)

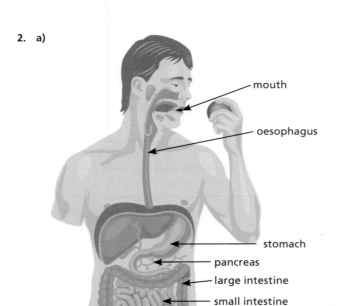

- mouth
- oesophagus
- stomach
- pancreas
- large intestine
- small intestine
- **rectum**
- anus   **[8]**

b) a) mouth – food broken into pieces
   b) oesophagus – food passes from mouth to stomach
   c) stomach – food mixed with acid and enzymes to help break it down
   d) pancreas – produces enzymes to break down food
   e) large intestine – water absorbed into blood stream
   f) small intestine – broken down food absorbed into blood stream
   g) rectum – waste material stored
   h) anus – waste material eliminated   **[8]**
3. feeding in animals involves eating food **[1]**; that is broken down **[1]** feeding in plants involves making food **[1]**; from simple substances, (by photosynthesis) **[2]**

State clearly whether you are writing about plants or animals.

Pages 16–23 **Revise Questions**

Page 17 Quick Test
1. aerobic
2. aerobic
3. anaerobic
4. anaerobic
5. alcohol

Page 19 Quick Test
1. support, protection, enables us to move, makes red blood cells
2. ligaments
3. tendons
4. Working against each other or in different directions.

Page 21 Quick Test
1. water + carbon dioxide $\xrightarrow[\text{chlorophyll}]{\text{light}}$ glucose + oxygen

2. Respiration uses glucose and oxygen to release energy and water and carbon dioxide are produced. In photosynthesis, carbon dioxide and water are converted into glucose and water using light energy.
3. have a large surface area to catch as much sunlight as possible; are green because of the chemical chlorophyll used in photosynthesis; have small holes called stomata on the underside of the leaf to let in carbon dioxide and let out oxygen; have tiny tubes called xylem to carry water and minerals up from the roots; have tiny tubes called phloem to carry glucose away for storage.

4. Plants make food and oxygen for animals. Animals make carbon dioxide for plants.
5. How different organisms rely upon each other for their survival.

Page 23 Quick Test
1. How energy moves through the food web.
2. Build-up of poisons towards the top of a food chain.
3. Variation is the differences between organisms. It increases the chances of survival when the environment changes.

Pages 24–25 **Review Questions**

Page 24
1. unicellular organisms need different structures to enable them to survive **[1]**; in different environments **[1]**

Look for key words. The key word in this question is 'explain'.

2. bone cell – skeletal system   **[1]**
    red blood cell – transport system   **[1]**
    nerve cell – nervous system   **[1]**
    sperm cell – reproductive system   **[1]**

Draw straight lines using a ruler.

3.

Part	Male	Female
Testis	✓	✗
Egg cell	✗	✓
Vagina	✗	✓
Sperm	✓	✗
Penis	✓	✗

[5]

4. insect pollinated flowers are brightly coloured **[1]**, have a scent **[1]** and produce nectar to attract insects **[1]**, *or* wind pollinated flowers are not designed to attract insects so are not brightly coloured **[1]**, do not have a scent **[1]** or produce nectar but do produce lots of pollen **[1]**.

[total of 3 marks]

Show clearly if your answer relates to insect or wind pollinated flowers.

5. They pollinate our crops **[1]** and without pollination there would be no crops to harvest **[1]**.
6. Place pollen grains on a microscope slide.   **[1]**
    Cover pollen grains with a cover slip.   **[1]**
    Place slide on the microscope stage.   **[1]**
    Switch on lamp or adjust mirror.   **[1]**
    Select lens for suitable magnification.   **[1]**
    Focus the image with the focusing knob.   **[1]**

Page 25
1. When we breathe in the ribs move up and out and the diaphragm moves down **[1]**. Pressure drops **[1]** and volume increases **[1]**. When we breathe out the ribs in and down and diaphragm moves up **[1]**. Pressure increases **[1]** and volume decreases **[1]**.
2. exercise; smoking; asthma   **[3]**
3. carbohydrates – provide energy   **[1]**
    fat – stores energy   **[1]**
    proteins – used to grow new cells   **[1]**
    vitamins – needed for chemical reactions to take place **[1]**
    minerals – needed for strong bones and blood   **[1]**
    fibre – speeds movement up through the gut   **[1]**
    water – dissolves chemicals for chemical reactions to take place **[1]**
4. Bacteria help break down food **[1]**, so it can be absorbed into the blood **[1]**.
5. It makes a reaction take place more quickly **[1]**, without being used up in the process **[1]**.

Learn definitions. They are an easy way to score marks.

6. The small intestine is where water is absorbed. **[1]**

Page 26
1. uses oxygen – aerobic [1]
   produces lactic acid – anaerobic [1]
   produces alcohol – anaerobic [1]
   releases the most energy – aerobic [1]
   fermentation – anaerobic [1]

   > Only write one tick in each row or you will not be given the marks.

2. In yeast it produces carbon dioxide [1], and alcohol [1].
   In humans it produces lactic acid [1].
3. The skeleton provides support for the body [1], enables movement to occur because of the joints [1], protects the brain heart and lungs [1], and makes red blood cells in the long bones [1].
4. 1 – skull; 2 – ribs; 3 – spine; 4 – elbow joint; 5 – hip joint; 6 – femur; 7 – kneecap; 8 – radius and ulna; 9 – pelvis; 10 – humerus [10]
5. Muscles can only contract [1], so two muscles are needed to move the joint in two different directions [1]. This is called an antagonistic pair [1].

   > Remember, muscles can only contract, they cannot expand.

Page 27
1. produces oxygen – photosynthesis [1]
   produces carbon dioxide – respiration [1]
   uses energy from sunlight – photosynthesis [1]
   releases energy – respiration [1]
   requires chlorophyll – photosynthesis [1]
2. any 5 of: very light; contains chlorophyll; has a large surface area; has holes to absorb carbon dioxide and release oxygen; has cells to carry water to the leaf and food away from the leaf [5]
3.

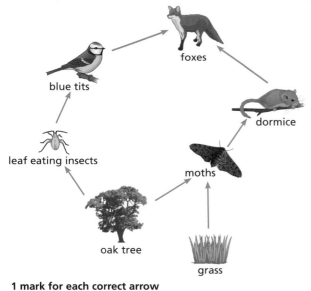

foxes
blue tits
dormice
leaf eating insects
moths
oak tree
grass

1 mark for each correct arrow [7]

> Always start with the plants and draw the arrows pointing away from them.

4. pollinate flowers [1]; may be a pest that destroy crops [1].
5. Bioaccumulation [1] occurs because large animals eat lots of small ones so the poison builds up [1].

Page 29 Quick Test
1. 23 from mum and 23 from dad
2. chromosome
3. A single instruction found on a chromosome.
4. James Watson, Francis Crick, Maurice Wilkins, Rosalind Franklin

Page 31 Quick Test
1. Continuous, e.g. height, where a range exists between very short and very tall with most being somewhere near the middle of the range. Discontinuous, e.g. blood groups, where distinct groups exist.
2. sexual reproduction
3. The range of different organisms in an ecosystem.
4. A place where genetic material is collected and stored.

Page 33 Quick Test
1. A substance that affects the human body.
2. An unwanted effect on the human body.
3. Any two from caffeine, nicotine and alcohol.
4. The need to keep taking the drug.

Page 35 Quick Test
1. any three from: eyes produce tears that contain a chemical to kill microbes; ears produce wax to trap microbes; nose and throat produce mucus to trap microbes; skin acts as a barrier to microbes; stomach produces acid to kill microbes in food; urine flushes out microbes that enter the genitals; vagina produces acid to kill microbes
2. bacteria; viruses; fungi
3. when dead microbes are injected into the body causing the blood to make memory cells
4. antibiotics do not work against viruses

Page 36
1. Aerobic respiration uses oxygen [1]. Anaerobic respiration produces lactic acid [1], produces alcohol [1], releases the least energy [1].
2. a) glucose; carbon dioxide [2]
   b) carbon dioxide; alcohol (can be either way round) [2]
   c) lactic acid [1]
3. Respiration releases energy [1] for all the chemical processes living things need [1].

Page 37
4. supports the body; helps with movement; protects some organs; makes red blood cells. [4]

   > This is a two mark question so you need to write two parts to your answer.

5. 1 = cartilage; 2 = lubricating fluid; 3 = ligament; 4 = tibia; 5 = femur [5]
6. a) contracts; bends arm [2]
   b) contracts; straightens arm [2]
   c) antagonistic [1]
1. a) carbon dioxide; oxygen [2]
   b) light; chlorophyll [2]
2. animals make carbon dioxide; plants use carbon dioxide; animals use oxygen; plants make oxygen [4]

Page 38
1. 46; 46; 23; 23; 46 [5]
2. A – cell, B – nucleus, C – chromosome, D – gene [4]

Page 39
3. Continuous variation shows a complete range of differences [1] but discontinuous variation has discrete groups of variation [1].
1.

ears – produce wax to trap microbes

eyes – produce tears that contain a chemical to kill microbes

nose and throat – produce mucus to trap microbes

skin – acts as a barrier to microbes

stomach – produces acid to kill microbes in food

vagina – produces acid to kill microbes

urine – flushes out microbes that enter the genitals

[7]
2. A medical drug is used to treat disease [1]. A recreational drug is used for pleasure [1].
3. A depressant relaxes the body [1], e.g. cannabis or heroin [1]. A stimulant makes you alert [1], e.g. cocaine or amphetamine [1]. A hallucinogen alters the perception of reality [1], e.g. LSD or magic mushrooms [1].
4. Drinking can cause liver failure [1] and increased risk of heart failure [1]. Smoking increases the risk of heart disease [1] lung cancer [1] and lung infections [1].

Page 41 Quick Test
1. Filter the mixture using filter paper. The residue in the filter paper is the solid.
2. small
3. The evaporated and re-condensed liquid following boiling a mixture.
4. Draw a line approximately 1 cm from the bottom of chromatography paper in pencil. Place a sample of each liquid mixture on the line. Place the paper into a beaker containing the solvent (e.g. water). As the solvent moves up the paper the more soluble pigments move further. Once the first pigment has reached the top, remove and dry the paper.

Page 43 Quick Test
1.

Solid	Liquid	Gas

2. Calcium carbonate decomposes into calcium oxide and carbon dioxide when it is heated.
3. Oxidation is when substances gain oxygen in a reaction.
4. Water and oxygen. The process is faster if salt is also present.

Page 45 Quick Test
1. CO_2 and H_2O
2. The number of protons in the nucleus of an atom of the element.
3. two
4. three

Page 47 Quick Test
1. nitrogen + oxygen ➜ nitrogen oxide
2. potassium sulfate

3. Three from: sonorous, shiny, malleable, conducts heat, conducts electricity, ductile, high melting point.
4. Three from: insulator (heat and electric), low melting points, gases at room temperature, low density.

Page 48
1. a) discontinuous [1]
   b) blood groups, tongue rolling [2]

Your teacher may give you other examples.

2. when the environment is changing very quickly [1]
3. a) Watson and Crick produced a theory to explain the structure of DNA [1]
   b) Rosalind Franklin produced evidence to support their theory [1]

Page 49
1. pathogen – disease-causing microbe [1]
   toxin – poison produced by a disease-causing microbe [1]
   antibody – chemical produced by white blood cells to kill pathogens [1]
2. bacteria – tuberculosis [1]
   virus – polio [1]
   fungus – athlete's foot [1]
   [1 mark for each named microbe with a disease caused by it]

Your teacher may give you other examples.

3. less addictive [1]
   less serious side effects [1]
4. Addiction is the need to take more and more of a drug [1]. Withdrawal is the physical effects on the body of not taking the drug [1].

Learn definitions. They are an easy way to score marks.

5. Drinking alcohol – liver failure [1]
   Smoking – lung cancer [1]
   Taking LSD – trying to fly off a tall building [1]
   Using heroin – reduces breathing [1]
6. some white cells can engulf microbes [1]; some white cells produce chemicals to destroy microbes [1]; some white cells called memory cells protect us from future infections [1]

Page 50
1. a) distillation [1]
   b) chromatography [1]
   c) filtration [1]
2. a) A and C [2]

Remember that elements that are gases at room temperature and pressure travel round as pairs.

   b) C [1]
3. Pour the sea water mixture into a filter funnel [1]. Allow the liquid to pass through [1]. Discard the residue and collect the filtrate [1]. Place the filtrate into an evaporating basin and heat [1]. Once the water has evaporated salt crystals will be left behind [1].

The key here is to say what will happen in steps. A little like writing a recipe.

4. Vinnie could measure the distance each pigment moved on the chromatogram [1] from the starting line [1].
5. The filter removes solid particles/waste/food that are building up in the water [1]. Filtration works by passing a liquid containing solid particles through a barrier that only allows small molecules through [1], leaving the larger particles behind [1].

Page 51
1. a) iii [1]
   b) ii [1]
2. ii; iii [2]
3. a) B [1]
   b) C [1]
   c) A [1]
4. An element is made up of only one kind of atom [1].
   A compound is made up of more than one different type of atom [1] chemically joined together [1].

Pages 52–59 Revise Questions

Page 53 Quick Test
1. In most solids the particles are closer together than in the liquid, therefore the density is greater.
2. Absolute zero (0 K) or −273 °C.
3. Sublimation is where a substance changes from a solid to a gas with no liquid phase.
4. Solids have all their particles touching and vibrating in position and have a defined shape. Liquids have at least 50% particles touching and move as well as vibrate and they take the shape of the container that they are in. Gases have no particles touching and will occupy all of the available space in a container.

Page 55 Quick Test
1. If the air in a sealed balloon is heated the gas particles will gain kinetic energy and move faster. This increases the air pressure, so the balloon will get bigger until the air pressure inside equals the air pressure outside. If the pressure becomes too great, the balloon may burst.
2. If the air in a sealed balloon is cooled the gas particles will lose kinetic energy and move more slowly. This decreases air pressure, so the balloon will get smaller until the pressure inside equals the air pressure outside.
3. Unlike other solids, the particles in ice are further apart than in a liquid. This means that there are fewer ice molecules in a given volume compared to the same volume of liquid water. The density of ice is therefore lighter, so it will float.
4. Diffusion occurs where particles at a higher concentration move randomly to areas where they are present in a lower concentration. The bigger the difference, the faster the rate of diffusion.

Page 57 Quick Test
1. A catalyst reduces the activation energy for a reaction, making it take place at lower energy levels than would normally be the case.
2. Activation energy is the minimum amount of energy needed to ensure that a reaction takes place.
3. A word equation just tells you what the reactants and products are, whereas a chemical equation tells you what atoms are present and the ratio of reactants and products.
4. (s), (l), (g), (aq)

Page 59 Quick Test
1. The substance is a weak acid, closer to being neutral than a strong acid.
2. Neutralisation is where an acid reacts with a base to form a pH 7 solution.
3. metal + acid ➔ salt + hydrogen
4. UI paper relies on using your eyes and judging the pH, a pH probe and a data logger measures the actual pH. So pH probe and a data logger is both more accurate and more reliable.

Pages 60–61 Review Questions

Page 60
1. a) sample A = 3; sample B = 2 [2]
   b) sample A [1]

c) The line is drawn in pencil because otherwise the line would move up the paper [1] along with the pigments being tested [1].
2. a) thermal decomposition [1]
   b) calcium carbonate ➔ calcium oxide + carbon dioxide [2]
3. C(s) + O_2(g) ➔ CO_2(g) [3]

[3 marks. 1 mark for correct reactants on left-hand side, 1 mark for correct product on right-hand side, and 1 mark for correct state symbols.]

Page 61
1. a) The circles (atoms) have been rearranged [1] and joined together in a new way [1].
   b) Substance Y is hydrogen [1]. Substance Z is water/dihydrogen oxide/H_2O [1].
   c) Mass has been conserved in the reaction because the number of atoms of each element is the same on both sides of the equation. [1]
2. A = sulfuric acid; B = magnesium nitrate; C = hydrochloric acid; D = hydrogen; E = lithium [4]
3. a) P;
   b) C;
   c) P;
   d) P;
   e) C [1]
4. 2Mg(s) + O_2(g) ➔ 2MgO(s) [1]

Although d) is balanced, it is incorrect as oxygen exists as O_2 molecules.

Pages 62–63 Practice Questions

Page 62
1. Solid should have at least 3 rows of atoms, all touching, with no gaps [1]. Liquid should have approximately 11 atoms, at least 50% of them touching, with gaps present [1]. Gas should have no atoms touching and show a random arrangement [1].
2. a) Sally would see blue air freshener appearing. [1]
   b) The air freshener is condensing back into a solid from a gas as it cools. [1]
3. Brownian motion is the process by which large particles are hit by the random collision of particles [1] causing the large particles to move in random directions [1].
4. When liquid, water molecules can fit closer together [1] than when they are arranged as a solid lattice structure [1]. This means that the ice is less dense than the liquid form of water [1].
5. b) The CO_2 gas particles are slowed down rapidly causing a solid to form.

Page 63
1. a) [2]

   b) copper oxide [1]
2. c [1]
3. metal + acid ➔ **salt + hydrogen** [1]
4. a) red [1]
   b) orange / yellow [1]
   c) green [1]
   d) blue / purple [1]
5. a) magnesium chloride + hydrogen [1]
   b) copper nitrate + water [1]
   c) vanadium sulfate + water + carbon dioxide [1]

Page 65 Quick Test
1. no
2. aluminium
3. anything above sodium in the reactivity series
4. The reactivity series is a list of the comparative reactivity of metals and carbon. It can be used to decide whether a displacement reaction will take place or not.

Page 67 Quick Test
1. They are unreactive, so when found would have been in their elemental form.
2. cool the clay very quickly
3. A combination of materials that, when bonded together, have new, enhanced properties.
4. chemically join monomer units together

Page 69 Quick Test
1. igneous, metamorphic and sedimentary
2. If the chemicals in the lithosphere were soluble, the rain would have washed them away millions of years ago.
3. Check your answer against the picture on p. 69.

Page 71 Quick Test
1. human activity
2. Rare or valuable parts of a product are extracted from waste and then used in a new product or process.
3.

4. Scientists believe that humans are causing climate change through activities such as burning fossil fuels, car use, cutting down rainforests, livestock farming, and paddy fields. The carbon dioxide released is causing the climate to heat up (the greenhouse effect).

Page 72
1. a) A [1]
   b) B [1]
   c) C [1]
2. a) The water molecules can get closer together when a liquid compared to when they are a solid [1]. This means that liquid water is denser than ice [1]. The liquid water at the bottom of the pond will not freeze [1].
   b) If Hilary switches the pump back on, the water will circulate [1] and so the water at the bottom will get colder [1] and possibly freeze [1].

Page 73
1. a) sodium + chlorine → sodium chloride,
   [1 mark for reactants, 1 mark for products]
   b) $2Na(s) + Cl_2(g) → 2NaCl(s)$ [2]
2. a) hydrogen peroxide → water + oxygen [2]
   b) a catalyst [1]

3. a)

[2]

   b) Before heating – a number of particles drawn, none touching. After heating – same number of particles drawn, further apart! [1]

Page 74
1. a) iron and tin [2]
   b) carbon + tin carbonate → **tin + carbon dioxide** [2]
2. monomers [1]
3. Basalt is an igneous rock that cooled very quickly [1]. This led to small crystals rather than large [1].
4. A composite is a substance that consists of different materials bonded together [1]. Has different properties to the individual substances alone. [1]

Page 75
1.

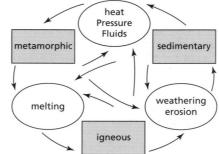

core
mantle
crust

[3]

2.

heat
Pressure
Fluids

metamorphic   sedimentary

melting   weathering erosion

igneous

[5]

3. a) unusual changes in normal weather patterns [1]
   b) ii and iv [2]
4. Recycling resources is important as the resources are in limited supply [1]. Recycling means that the resources are available for use in other products [1].

Page 77 Quick Test
1. unbalanced
2. the Newton (N)
3. Force arrows indicate the direction and strength of a force.
4. force x distance in a given direction; or moment is the turning effect of the force

Page 79 Quick Test
1. m/s or Km/s
2. Work is when an object changes speed or shape.
3. 1.2 km/min or 0.02 km/s or 72 km/h or 20 m/s

Page 81 Quick Test

1. Mass is the amount of particles that make up an object (measured in kg). Weight is a force on the object due to gravity (measured in N).
2. The Earth has gravitational field strength due to its mass. The further away from the centre of mass, the less it will affect an object.
3. An electric field.
4.

repelling   attracting

Page 83 Quick Test

1. Atmospheric pressure is due to the weight of air molecules pushing down on the surface. The higher you go, the fewer air molecules there are, therefore less to push down and so less pressure.
2. N/m^2
3. 1000 N
4. The upthrust from the water.

Pages 84–85 **Review Questions**

Page 84

1. gold [1]
2. a) ii; iv [2]
   b) ii) iron + copper sulfate → iron sulfate + copper [1]
      iv) copper + silver nitrate → copper nitrate + silver [1]
3. Iron ore is heated at a high temperature with carbon [1]. The carbon displaces the iron, which pours out of the bottom of the furnace [1]. The carbon reacts with oxygen to form waste carbon dioxide [1].

Page 85

1.

Rock Type	Description
Igneous	is very hard and made of lots of small crystals
Sedimentary	has layers of crystals
Metamorphic	has veins, has a waxy appearance, and is often used for statues

[3]

2.

Element	Abundance (%)
Oxygen	46
Silicon	28
Aluminium	0.8
Iron	0.5

[4]

3. a) Arwen and Ruth [1]
   b) Recycling does use energy [1]. However, the materials are rare and there would be a greater cost in trying to find more and extracting them [1]. It is really a question of using less energy [1]. [2 of the 3 possible marks]

Pages 86–87 Practice Questions

Page 86

1. B (8 N) [1]
2. a) 200 g [1]
   b) 150 g [1]
3. 60 s + 48 s = 108 s,
   800 m/108 s = 7.4 m/s [2]
4. 15 N x 10 cm = 150 Ncm or 15 N x 0.1 m =1.5 Nm [3]

Page 87

1. a) S N N S or N S S N [2]
   b) Turn one of the magnets the other way round [1] so the poles are opposite to one another [1].
2. 10 kg – 100 N, 15.5 kg – 155 N, 2000 g – 20 N [3]

> Watch out for the units. The last mass is in g not kg.

3. a)

[1]

   b) The pressure on the water is greatest for the lowest hole. The pressure decreases towards the top of the bottle [1], so B will have less pressure than C, but more than A. A has the least pressure [1].
4. Amy 2.4 N/m
   George 1.7 N/m [2]

Pages 88–95 Revise Questions

Page 89 Quick Test

1. 1 N upwards
2. A distance–time graph can tell us how far an object travelled over a set time. This also enables speed to be calculated.
3. 130 mph
4. Whether the object is accelerating or decelerating slowly or rapidly.

Page 91 Quick Test

1. 12 h
2. because the Earth is tilted on its axis so the hemispheres receive different amounts of radiation from the Sun.
3. 2000 N
4. Mercury must be smaller in mass and so have lower gravitational field strength.

Page 93 Quick Test

1. fuel + oxygen → carbon dioxide + water + energy
2. Combustion is a much faster reaction, with the energy released producing heat and/or light. Respiration is very slow in comparison.
3. Radiation is the transfer of heat via waves (infrared).
4. 1000 J

Page 95 Quick Test

1. 50 Hz is 50 waves per second
2. An echo is a reflected sound wave.
3. To reduce echoes, place angled materials (like egg boxes) on the walls so that the waves from a singer or instrument are not reflected back.
4. A loudspeaker converts music to an electrical signal which causes electromagnets to move a fabric skin. This movement makes air particles move as sound waves which then reach the ear.

Pages 96–97 Review Questions

Page 96

1. a) no [1]
   b) yes [1]
   c) no [1]
2. 600 g – stretch was 12 cm; [1]
   700 g – stretch was 14 cm [1]
3. Speed = distance ÷ time
   27600 km/h = 42927 km ÷ time [1]
   time = 42927 km ÷ 27600 km/h [1]
       = 1.56 h (or 93.3 min) [1]

Page 97

1. c and d [2]
2. **a)** The rod has been charged with electrons / had electrons removed by rubbing **[1]** and the water, which must have the opposite charge, is attracted to it **[1]**.
   b) it will be repelled (as it has the same charge). [1]
3. The ship does not completely sink **[1]** as, although it is submerged under water, the downward force of the weight **[1]** is counterbalanced by the upthrust or reaction force of the water **[1]**.

Pages 98–99 Practice Questions

Page 98

1. A – Lisa jogged for 4 min; B – Lisa stopped for 2 min; C – Lisa walked for 8 min; D – Lisa stopped for 3 min [4]
2. 80 km/h [1]
3. **a)** an astronomical unit of distance, the distance that light travels in an Earth year [1]
   b) 1 light year = 300,000 km/s x 60 x 60 x 24 x 365
   = 9,460,800,000,000 km [1]
   4.2 light years = 9,460,800,000,000 km x 4.2 [1]
   = 39,735,360,000,000 km [1]
   Accept answer rounded to 40,000,000,000,000 km
4.

east   west [2]

Page 99

1. **a)** Just when cord goes taut. [1]
   b) As he steps off the bridge, but before he starts falling. [1]
2. **a)** A = oxygen; B = carbon dioxide; C = water [2 marks for all 3 correct]
   b) respiration [1]
3. c) radiation [1]
4. Jamie and Linda can hear each other because the sound waves are reflected **[1]** by the walls and also spread in all directions from their voices **[1]**.

Pages 100–107 Revise Questions

Page 101 Quick Test

1. R = V/I so R = 1.5 V/3 A = 0.5 Ω
2. the ohm (Ω)
3. An insulator is a substance that offers complete resistance to electric current. It does not conduct electricity.
4.

Series circuit

Parallel circuit

Page 103 Quick Test

1. increase number of coils, increase current, add an iron core
2. The Earth is like a bar magnet because it creates a North and a South pole and the field lines around the Earth resemble those of a bar magnet.
3. The closer the magnetic field lines, the stronger the magnetic field.
4. cobalt, iron and nickel

Page 105 Quick Test

1. light waves do not need a medium to travel through, so they can travel much faster
2. a ripple tank
3. light = 300,000,000 m/s and sound = 300 m/s so light travels approximately 1,000,000 times faster
4. Waves in phase add together, so increase in size (amplitude).

Page 107 Quick Test

1. violet
2. a prism
3. Light enters into the pinhole and forms an upside down image on the back of the camera. This is where the film would be placed if the image needed to be recorded.
4. where the light hits an uneven surface and reflects in different directions

Pages 108–109 Review Questions

Page 108

1. d) travelling at 60 km/h [1]
2. **a)** gravity / gravitational pull from the Sun [1]
   b) 300,000 km/s x 60 x 60 = 1,080,000,000 km/h
   4.1 h x 1,080,000,000 km/h = 4,428,000,000 km [3]
3. The Earth has seasons because the planet is tilted **[1]** in respect to the North Star. This means that, as the Earth goes around the Sun the summer is when a hemisphere is tilted towards the Sun **[1]** and winter is when a hemisphere is tilted away from the Sun **[1]**.

Page 109

1. **a)** i and iv [2]
   b) iv [1]
2. **a)** As we get older we lose our ability to hear higher pitched/ high frequency sounds **[1]**. Hence teenagers can hear the noise, but the adults cannot **[1]**.
   b) The loudspeaker vibrates **[1]**, hitting air particles which gain energy **[1]**. They move in waves to the teenager's ear **[1]**. The eardrum vibrates at the same frequency as the original sound **[1]**.
3. b) The bomber absorbs the radar signal. [1]

Pages 110–111 Practice Questions

Page 110

1.

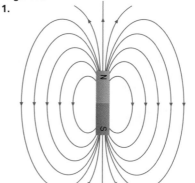

[2]

2. **a)** i; iv; vi [3]
   b) the electromagnet can be turned on and off [1]

3. A2 and A3 = 2 A, A4 = 4 A [2]
4. **a)** P = I x V so I = P/V =
60 W / 230 V = 0.26 A [1]
   b) 60 x 200 = 12,000 Wh = 12 kWh [3]

Page 111
1.

[3]

2. **a)**

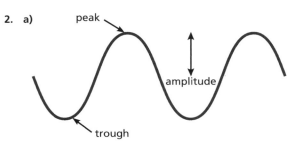

[3]
   b) 2 Hz [2]
3. red, orange, yellow, green, blue, indigo, violet (top to bottom on diagram) [4]

Pages 112–113 **Review Questions**

Page 112
1. c) cobalt [1]
2. C [1]
3. **a)** it will turn on/activate and attract the armature [1]
   b) it will be attracted to the electromagnet [1] and complete the second circuit [1]

Page 113
1. In a mirror, all the waves are reflected at the same angle [1]. This is specular reflection [1]. With paper, the rays hit the uneven surface and reflect in different directions. This is called scattered diffusion [1].
2. **a)** 10 Hz means 10 waves per second [1]
   b) Four added waves [1] same wavelength [1] (See diagram below)
   c) Four added waves reflected from the bar [1] same wavelength as incoming waves [1] (See diagram below)

3. **a)**

[3]

   b) refraction [1]

Pages 114–125 **Mixed Test-Style Questions**

Page 114
1. **a)** **i)** B should be drawn at the top of the apparatus, inside the round bottomed flask. [1]
       ii) The distillate is the liquid collected at the end of the distillation tube. The label X should appear in the liquid, or be clearly labelled with a line to the collected liquid. [1]
   b) The cold water enters at the bottom of the distillation tube and leaves at the top [1]. This is so that the gas will always encounter colder conditions as it moves down the distillation tube. This means it will condense more rapidly. [1]
   c) 9 [1]
   d) Point Y is a liquid. At least 11 particles need to be drawn with at least 50% of the particles touching; Point Z is a gas. A minimum of five particles need to be drawn with no particles touching **[both diagrams need to be drawn correctly for 1 mark].**
2. **a)** 20 N [1]
   b) Michael is already using 20 N of force. Kerrie weighs 600 N, so 600 N / 2 = 300 N. Therefore 320 N of force used. [2]
   If part (a) is incorrect and in part (b) only uses 600 N, follow through and accept 300 N   (with working).
   If part (a) is correct but in part (b) only uses 600 N, award 1 mark for working.
   c) **i)** pressure = force / area
       Force = 650 N. The area of 1 stilt is 9 cm². There are 2 stilts. Therefore total area = 2 x 9 cm² = 0.0018 m².
       650 N / 0.0018 = 361,111.1 N/m²
       [1 mark for correct working, 1 mark for correct answer]
       If working shows only 9 cm² used, award maximum 1 mark.
       ii) To exert less pressure she needs to use stilts with a larger surface area or lose weight. [1]
3. **a)** Breathing in is shown by the rubber sheet being pulled down [1]; volume in the bottle increases [1] and pressure decreases so air enters the balloons [1]. Breathing out is shown by the rubber sheet going up [1], volume decreases [1], pressure increases and forces air out of the balloons [1].
   b) **i)** asthma [1]
       ii) smoker [1]
       iii) normal [1]
   c) **i)** 10→8; 10→6; 8→6 [3]

Diffusion always moves from high to low concentration.

       ii) Glucose moves by diffusion [1] from a high concentration [1] to a low concentration [1].
   d) **i)** anaerobic makes lactic acid or aerobic doesn't make lactic acid [1];
       aerobic releases more energy or anaerobic releases less energy [1]
       ii) humans produce lactic acid [1]; yeast produces alcohol [1]

Remember *aerobic* uses oxygen in *air*.

4. **a)** A new material has been deposited on the surface of the nail. [1]
   b) iron + oxygen + water [1] → iron hydroxide [1]

c) Naveen's hypothesis would have been: an iron nail will only rust if water and oxygen are present / an iron nail will not rust if either water or oxygen are missing. **[2]**

d) i) Naveen would see a reddish–brown metal forming on the nail **[1]**. She would also see the blue colour disappearing / a green solution forming **[1]**. [**Accept the colour of the nail has changed**]

   ii) iron displaced the copper from the sulfate and takes its place **[1]**; iron is higher in the reactivity series than copper **[1]**

5. a) Numbers of blue tits reduce **[1]** because fewer insects would be available to eat **[1]**. Numbers of moths increase **[1]** because there is less competition for their food from the leaf-eating insects **[1]**.

This question is about interdependence, i.e. how one organism in a food web affects another organism.

b)

	✓ or ✗
Respiration stores energy as light	✗
Photosynthesis uses energy from light	✓
Respiration breaks down large molecules to smaller molecules	✓
Photosynthesis creates organic molecules from inorganic molecules	✓
Respiration releases energy from chlorophyll	✗
Photosynthesis stores energy as light	✗

[6]

c) i) extinction means all members of a species have died out worldwide **[1]**

Remember, once an organism is extinct it cannot return.

   ii) a change in their environment **[1]** which happened rapidly **[1]**

d)

[1 mark for both correct]

e) Most scientific discoveries are the result of a scientist building on the work of a previous scientist **[1]**. Scientists have their results checked by other scientists **[1]**. Scientists use data from experiments to check their ideas **[1]**.

6. a) i) Carriage X should have S–N; carriage Z should show N–S. **OR** carriage X should have N–S; carriage Z should show S–N. **All poles need to be correct, none missing.** **[1]**

   ii) Carriage X would now be attracted to carriage Y, whereas carriage Z would repel carriage Y **[1]** this is because opposite poles attract and like poles repel **[1]**.

b) A, steel; B, magnet; C, aluminium **[2 marks for all 3 correct, 1 mark for 2 correct, no marks for only 1 correct]**.

c) cobalt and iron should be ticked **[1]**

Glossary

a

absorb (*in physics*) waves of light taken in by a material and not reflected

abundance how available a substance is

abuse misuse of a drug

acid a compound containing hydrogen that can be replaced by a metal to form a salt

activation energy the amount of energy that has to be available before a chemical reaction can take place

addiction the need to keep taking a drug

aerobic respiration that uses oxygen

air pressure the force due to gases acting on an area

alkali soluble form of a base

alveoli small air sacs in the lungs

amplitude the maximum displacement of a wave from zero

anaemia deficiency disease caused by a lack of iron

anaerobic respiration that does not use oxygen

antagonistic pair two muscles that move a joint in different directions

anther male part of a flower that produces pollen

antibiotic a drug that kills some types of bacteria

antibody chemical produced by our body to destroy a microorganism

anus exit of the digestive system

asthma a condition that makes breathing difficult

atom the smallest component of an element that retains the element's chemical properties

attraction (*in physics*) the electric or magnetic force that acts between bodies with an opposite charge

b

bacteria a type of microorganism

base a solid chemical that reacts with an acid to form a salt and water

bioaccumulation build-up of toxic materials in a food web

biodiversity the range of different species in an ecosystem or the range of variation in a species

Brownian motion the random movement of particles in a fluid (liquid or gas) due to collisions with the atoms or molecules in the fluid

c

carbohydrate foods such as starch and sugar

carbon cycle a sequence where carbon is exchanged among the different spheres of the Earth (the atmosphere, lithosphere, hydrosphere and biosphere)

cartilage tissue that cushions the ends of bones at a joint

catalyst a chemical that lowers the activation energy of a reaction without being used up in the process

cell wall the supporting wall around a plant cell

ceramic a non-metallic solid that has been altered through heating

chemical potential energy the amount of energy stored in chemical bonds. This is released during combustion or respiration.

chemical reaction representation of a chemical reaction using the chemical formulae of the reactants and products

chlorophyll green chemical found in plants that aids photosynthesis

chloroplast place where chlorophyll is stored

chromosome a long strand of DNA

combustion the chemical reaction between fuel and oxygen

composite two or more substances with different properties that, when combined, form a new material with different properties

compression reduction in volume as a result of a pushing force

concentration the abundance of a substance in a given volume

condense to turn from a gas to a liquid

conductor   has a low resistance to the flow of electric current or heat energy

consensus   broad agreement

continuous variation   variation that occurs across a range

consumers   animals which consume food for energy

convex   a lens which is thickest in the middle

cytoplasm   the place where chemical reactions take place in a cell

d

DC motor   a motor that can be run on direct current

density   the amount of mass per unit volume

diaphragm   domed shaped muscle used during breathing

diffusion   (*in chemistry*) the process whereby molecules in a liquid or gas mix as a result of their random motion; (*in biology*) movement of molecules from a high to a low concentration

discontinuous variation   variation that occurs in distinct groups

dispersal   spreading of seeds over a wide area

displace the action of one metal replacing another in a compound

distillate the collected liquid resulting from evaporation and then condensation in distillation apparatus

DNA   chemical that codes for life

drug   a substance that changes the body

ductile   capable of being drawn into wires

e

echo   a reflected sound wave arriving back some time after the sound was originally made

ecosystem   a system of interacting organisms that live in one area

egg cell   female cell used for reproduction

electric field   generated by electrically charged particles in a varying magnetic field

electromagnet   a temporary magnet created by an electric current running through a wire

element   a substance made up of only one type of atom, having the same number of protons in each nucleus

embryo   a group of cells that will grow into a baby

environment   the surroundings in a habitat

equilibrium   where both potential states of a system are equal

equinox   the day when day and night are the same length

evaporation   when a liquid turns into a gas

extinction   when all the members of a species are dead

f

fat   a type of food that is used to store energy

fermentation   the process of anaerobic respiration in yeast

fertile   able to reproduce using sexual reproduction

fertilisation   the joining together of a male and female sex cell

fibre   indigestible material found in food

field lines   demonstrate where a magnetic field is present

filtrate   the liquid which passes through filter paper

filtration   a method of separating an insoluble solid from a liquid

food chain   picture showing which organisms eat each other in a habitat

food web   many food chains linked together

force   a push or pull resulting from the interaction between two objects

fossil fuels   high energy substances made from the remains of plants and animals that died millions of years ago that have been subjected to immense pressure and high temperatures

frequency   number of waves per second. Measured in Hz

fungi   a type of microorganism

g

gene   a single instruction found on a chromosome

gestation   time period from fertilisation to birth

glucose   food produced by photosynthesis

gravitational field strength   the strength of an object's gravitational pull on objects

gravitational potential energy the amount of energy an object has due to its position in a gravitational field. The higher the object, the more energy

group (*in chemistry*) a column of elements in the periodic table

h

heredity how characteristics are passed from one generation to the next

i

igneous rock formed when magma cools and solidifies

immune system system in our bodies that protects us from invading microorganisms

inheritance how characteristics are passed from one generation to the next

insulator does not conduct heat and/or electric current

interdependent organisms which depend upon one another for their survival

interspecific variation variation between species

interference where waves are out of sync they can either cancel or enhance each other

intestine the tube that goes from the stomach to the anus

intraspecific variation variation within a species

j

joint where two bones are held together to allow movement

joule the unit of energy

k

kinetic energy the energy possessed by an object due to its motion

kwashiorkor a protein deficiency disease

l

lactic acid waste substance produced by anaerobic respiration in humans

ligament tissue that holds two bones together at a joint

light year an astronomical unit of distance representing the distance light travels in an Earth year

longitudinal (*in physics*) disturbances that move in the direction of travel

m

magnetic field the area around a magnet where it can affect other magnetic materials

malleable capable of being hammered into shape without cracking

medicine a drug used to treat or prevent disease

membrane controls what goes into and what leaves a cell

memory cell a type of white blood cell produced after vaccination that produces antibodies to destroy that type of invading microorganism

menstruation monthly loss of tissue from the lining of a uterus

metamorphic rock that is transformed by high temperature and pressure

minerals chemicals needed by our body

mitochondria place where energy is released inside a cell (respiration takes place)

moment a force multiplied by the distance to a pivot

monomer a building block of a polymer

n

nectar sweet substance in flowers that attracts insects

neutral a chemical that is neither an acid nor a base

neutralisation the process by which an acid is neutralised by a base leading to a solution with pH 7

Newton the unit of force

niches small areas within an ecosystem

nucleus part of a cell that contains the DNA

o

observer (*in physics*) a person making an observation from a particular frame of reference

oesophagus a tube that connects the mouth to the stomach

organ a group of different tissues working together

organ system a group of organs working together

ovary   place where female sex cells are made

oxidation   the gain of oxygen in a chemical reaction

oxygen   gas given out by green plants

p

pancreas   organ that produces digestive enzymes

parallel   in a circuit this means that the circuit branches

pathogen   disease-causing organism

peak   (*in physics*) the top of the wave

period   a horizontal row on the periodic table

photosynthesis   the process by which plants make food (glucose)

pivot   the point of rotation of a lever

plimsoll line   drawn on a ship to indicate how deep the hull of the ship is submerged

pollination   transfer of pollen from one flower to another

polymer   a substance made of many monomers chemically joined together

pressure   the ratio of force to the area or volume over which the force is applied

producers   plants which produce food by photosynthesis

products   new chemicals formed as a result of a chemical reaction

protein   food used for growing new cells

pyramid of numbers   the number of each organism in a food chain shown as a horizontal bar chart. The wider the bar, the more organisms there are

r

reactants   the chemicals that react together in a chemical reaction

reaction force   the force exerted on an object countering the gravitational force of that object

reactivity   a measure of how easily a chemical reacts with other chemicals

recreational drug   a drug used for pleasure

rectum   last part of the digestive system where water is absorbed

recycling   collecting, extracting and then using for another purpose to avoid waste of useful materials

reduction   the loss of oxygen from a molecule

reflection   the bouncing of a wave off a surface

refraction   the apparent bending of light as it moves between mediums with different optical densities

relative   (*in physics*) the description given to where an observer is in relation to a scenario, e.g. watching two cars passing on the road or being in one of the cars

repulsion   the electric or magnetic force that acts between bodies with the same charge

resistance   the opposition of a component to the electric current running through it, leading to the transfer of energy

respiration   breaking down food to release energy

rust   the product of the reaction between iron, oxygen and water

s

salt   the name given to the product formed by swapping the hydrogen in an acid with a metal

scurvy   a disease caused by a lack of vitamin C

sedimentary   rock type formed by the settling of layers of material followed by extreme pressure

series   a circuit which is in a single loop, with no branches

side effect   an unwanted effect of a drug on the body

solstice   the longest or shortest day

solvent   a liquid into which solutes can dissolve

species   a group of organisms that reproduce to produce fertile offspring

speed   how far an object travels divided by the time travelled

sperm   male cell used for reproduction

stigma   female part of a flower where pollen is deposited

stoma   small hole on the underside of a leaf

stomach   a bag-shaped organ that helps digest food

stomata   lots of small holes on the underside of leaves

sublimation   transformation from a solid to a gas, missing out the liquid state

t

tendon   tissue that attaches muscle to bone

testes   place where male sex cells are made

thermal decomposition   breakdown of a compound into products when heated

tissue   a group of the same type of cells

toxin   substance poisonous to humans

transverse   moving side to side at right angles to the direction of travel. Transverse waves look like a repeating sideways S

u

ultrasound   sound with a frequency of over 20,000 Hz

unicellular   organism that consists of just one cell

upthrust   a specific type of reaction force, the counterforce of water to the weight of an object in water

uterus   place where a baby grows inside a woman

v

vaccination   a means of making the body produce antibodies to destroy an invading microorganism

vacuole   storage space inside a plant cell

variation   differences between different organisms

vibration   the movement of an object back and forth from an equilibrium position

virus   a type of microorganism

vitamins   essential nutrients needed in small amounts by the body to work properly

w

weight   the force of a mass in a gravitational field

word equation   representation of a chemical equation using the names of the reactants and products

work   the transfer of energy as an object moves in the direction of the force

Index

Collins

KS3 Revision
Science

Science

KS3

Workbook

Byron Dawson and
Eliot Attridge

Contents

KS3 Science Workbook

Contents

Biology

Cells – the Building Blocks of Life

1 The diagrams show a plant cell and an animal cell.

Complete the labels for each type of cell.

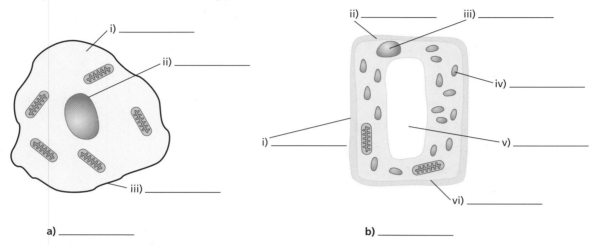

i) _____

ii) _____

iii) _____

a) _____

ii) _____   iii) _____

iv) _____

i) _____

v) _____

vi) _____

b) _____   [11]

2 Substances move in and out of cells by diffusion.

Put a tick (✓) in the box next to the statement about diffusion that is correct.

Oxygen and carbon dioxide move in and out of cells by diffusion	
Diffusion is when molecules move from where there are only a few of them to where there are many	
Diffusion only works when the Sun is shining	
Diffusion only takes place in animal cells, and not plant cells	

[1]

3 The diagram shows the movement of sugar molecules by diffusion between three different cells.

Write one number in each cell to show the relative concentration of sugar molecules in the three cells.

Choose from these three numbers: **10**   **15**   **20**

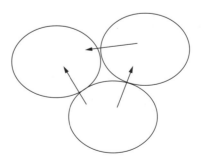

[2]

4 Draw a straight line to join the **part of cell** to its correct **job**.

Then complete the box labelled **found in** with either **animal, plant** or **both**.

The first one has been done for you.

Job	Part of cell	Found in...
Makes food from light energy	Nucleus	both
Stores DNA	Cell wall	
Supports the cell	Cell membrane	
Controls what enters and leaves the cell	Cytoplasm	
Where chemical reactions take place	Vacuole	
Provides support to the cell	Chloroplast	

[5]

5 Different cells do different jobs.

Write down the names of three different cells found in the human body and describe the job that each cell does.

[3]

6 Put the following words in the order that they happen.

The first one has been done for you.

birth   fertilisation   gametes produced   gestation

gametes produced _____ [3]

7 Look at the diagram of a flower.

State how the flower is pollinated.

[1]

Biology

1 The gas exchange system in humans consists of several parts.

Draw a straight line to connect each **part** with its correct **function**.

Part	Function
Diaphragm	Muscles that raise and lower the ribs
Bronchioles	Small air sacs where gas exchange takes place
Alveoli	Tubes that carry air in and out of the lungs
Intercostal muscles	Muscles that contract to breathe in

[3]

2 Read these statements about how humans breathe.

Put ticks (✓) in the boxes next to the **two** correct statements.

The diaphragm lowers when we breathe out	
When the lungs increase in volume the pressure drops	
When the pressure drops we breathe out	
When the ribs are raised we breathe out	
Oxygen diffuses from the alveoli into the blood	

[2]

3 Asthma affects the ability to breathe.

Put a tick (✓) in the box next to the correct statement about asthma.

Asthma reduces the number of air sacs	
Asthma increases the volume of the lungs	
Asthma causes the airways to narrow	
Asthma is improved by smoking	

[1]

4 A balanced diet contains different types of substances.

Draw straight lines to join each **substance** with the **reason** our body needs it.

Substance	Reason
Carbohydrates and fats	Dissolves chemicals so that chemical reactions can take place
Protein	Needed for strong bones and teeth
Vitamins	Used to help chemical reactions take place
Minerals	Used for growth and new tissue
Water	Gives our body energy

[4]

5 The following words are all parts of the digestive system.

Put them in the order in which food passes through them. The first has been done for you.

anus   large intestine   mouth   oesophagus   rectum   small intestine   stomach

mouth ....

....

[5]

6 Which of these statements about parts of the digestive system are true?

Put a tick (✓) in the box next to the **three** correct answers.

The anus is where the process of digestion starts	
The large intestine is where water is absorbed	
The mouth is where acid is added to our food	
The oesophagus connects the stomach to the small intestine	
The pancreas produces enzymes to help digest food	
The rectum is where food is broken down from large to small pieces	
The small intestine is where most food is broken down chemically	
The stomach is where waste material is eliminated	

[3]

Total Marks .... / 18

Biology

1 Which of these statements is the correct definition of respiration?

Put a tick (✓) in the box next to the correct answer.

Making food from water and carbon dioxide	
Using energy from the Sun to make food	
Using chlorophyll to store energy	
Releasing energy from food	
Breaking food down into simple molecules	

[1]

2 Write down the word equation for anaerobic respiration in humans.

....

[3]

3 Draw straight lines to match the **type** of respiration with each correct **description**.

Type	Description

Type

Aerobic

Anaerobic

Description

Releases the most energy

Produces lactic acid

Produces alcohol

Uses oxygen

[4]

4 Where does the energy released from food originally come from?

Put a tick (✓) in the box next to the correct answer.

Water ☐

Sunlight ☐

Carbon dioxide ☐

Chlorophyll ☐

[1]

5 The human skeleton does several different jobs.

Put crosses (**✗**) in the boxes next to the jobs **not done** by the human skeleton.

Supports the body	
Digests food	
Acts as a framework so muscles can make us move	
Transports nerve impulses around the body	
Protects some important organs	
Pumps blood around the body	
Makes red blood cells	

[3]

6 Look at this diagram of a joint found in the human skeleton.

Complete the labels.

Choose from these words, each word can be used more than once:

bone   cartilage   fluid   ligament   muscle   tendon

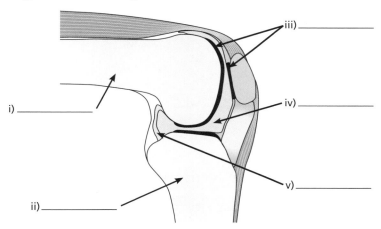

i) _____

ii) _____

iii) _____

iv) _____

v) _____

[5]

7 Muscles make the skeleton move.

Explain why each joint needs at least two muscles to make the joint work.

_____

_____

_____

_____

_____

[3]

Total Marks _____ / 20

Biology

1 Complete the word equation for photosynthesis below.

Use these words.

chlorophyll   carbon dioxide   glucose   light   oxygen   water

....

.... + ... ➔ .... + ...

.... [3]

2 The diagram below shows the inside of a leaf.

Complete the labels, using these words:

chloroplasts   lower epidermis   upper epidermis   stoma

i) _____

ii) _____

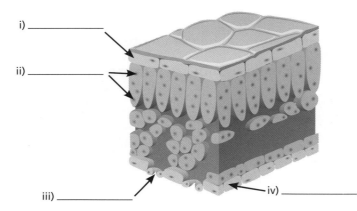

iii) _____   iv) _____ [3]

3 Read these statements.

Some of the statements describe how a leaf is adapted for photosynthesis.

Put a tick (✓) in the **three** boxes that best describe these adaptations.

Some leaves can be eaten by animals	
Birds can build their nests using leaves	
Leaves have a large surface area	
Chlorophyll is found in leaves	
There are small holes on the underside of leaves	
Leaves are made from cells	

[3]

4 Animals and plants are interdependent.

Put ticks (✓) in the boxes next to the **two** statements that, when used together, best describe this interdependence.

Animals use oxygen and produce carbon dioxide	
Some animals eat other animals	
Plants store energy in food	
Plants can use energy from stored food	
Some animals are eaten by other animals	
Plants use carbon dioxide and produce oxygen	

[2]

5 Look at the diagram of a food web.

Give **two food chains** using only information shown in the food web.

....

....

....

....

....

....

....

....

....

....

[2]

sparrowhawk

fox

slug

thrush

rabbit

lettuce

6 Look at the following list.

Put a tick (✓) in the box next to the word that describes what is transferred through a food web.

Oxygen ☐

Sugar ☐

Carbon dioxide ☐

Energy ☐

Water ☐

[1]

Total Marks .... / 14

Biology

1 Genetic information is inherited from our parents.

Choose **two** statements which, when taken together, best describe this process.

A	Sperm can swim
B	The nucleus contains DNA
C	Sperm and ova each contain 23 chromosomes
D	Genes are sections of DNA
E	Ova are female eggs
F	Fertilisation is when sperm and ova join together

_____ and _____   [2]

2 Order the following structures from largest to smallest.

cell   **chromosome**   **gene**   **nucleus**

_____   [3]

3 Draw straight lines to join each **structure** with the best **description** of its job.

Structure	Description
Chromosome	A length of DNA that is just one code for a protein
Gene	A strand of DNA made up of genes
Nucleus	Found in a cell and contains all the chromosomes

[2]

4 Different scientists were involved in the discovery of DNA.

Draw straight lines to join each **scientist** with their part in the **discovery**.

Scientist	Discovery
Watson and Crick	Made X-ray images of DNA
Maurice Wilkins	Produced evidence to support Watson and Crick's theory
Rosalind Franklin	Developed a theory for the structure of DNA

[2]

5 There are two types of variation, continuous and discontinuous.

Draw straight lines joining each **type of variation** with the correct **examples**.

Type of variation

Continuous

Discontinuous

Example

Height

Blood groups

Weight

Ability to roll tongue

[4]

6 Variation is important for the survival of a species.

Put ticks (✓) in the boxes next to the **two** statements that best explain why.

Variation increases the rate of evolution	
When the environment changes some members of the species will be more likely to survive	
Evolution does not happen when the environment changes	
Animals and plants compete for resources	
Members of the species that survive will breed to produce more offspring	
A shortage of resources causes animals and plants to die	

[2]

7 Explain what is meant by biodiversity.

_____

_____

[1]

8 Which of the following statements best describes a **gene bank**?

A	A place where clothes can be exchanged
B	A factory where genes are copied and sold
C	A cell that contains over a thousand different genes
D	A place where seeds from plants are stored

[1]

Total Marks .... / 17

Biology

Our Health and the Effects of Drugs

1 Which of these statements is the best definition of a drug?

Put a tick (✓) in the box next to the best answer.

A substance that is addictive	
A substance that affects the body	
A substance prescribed by a doctor	
A substance that is made from plants	
A substance that is illegal if it is not a medicine	

[1]

2 Some drugs are used to treat disease.

Many of these drugs have a side effect.

Give the definition of a side effect.

.... [1]

3 Which of these statements about white blood cells are true?

Put ticks (✓) in the boxes next to the correct answers.

White blood cells carry oxygen around the body ☐

White blood cells can engulf microbes ☐

White blood cells produce chemicals to kill microbes ☐

White blood cells stop microbes from getting into the blood ☐

White blood cells make the blood clot ☐

White blood cells produce chemicals to thin the blood ☐

[2]

4 Complete the following sentence by underlining the correct words.

Cigarettes contain *nicotine / aspirin*, which *speeds up / slows down* heart rate and *raises / lowers* blood pressure. [3]

5 Vaccines can prevent some diseases. Which of these statements about vaccination are true?

Put ticks (✓) in the boxes next to the correct answers.

Vaccines contain antibodies	
Vaccines contain white blood cells	
Vaccines cause the production of memory cells	
Vaccines contain antibiotics	
Vaccines contain dead disease-causing organisms	

[2]

6 Explain what is meant by a **recreational drug**.

.... [1]

7 Explain what is meant by a **medical drug**.

.... [1]

8 Some people think that cannabis should be made legal. Others disagree.

Write down reasons for both sides of this argument.

....

....

....

....

.... [2]

9 Complete the following sentences by underlining the **correct words**:

Drugs which make you feel awake and alert are called *depressants / stimulants / hallucinogens*. Some drugs can make people think they can see things that are not there. They are called *depressants / stimulants / hallucinogens*. An example of a depressant drug is *cannabis / amphetamine / LSD*. [3]

Total Marks .... / 16

Chemistry

Mixing, Dissolving and Separating

1 The following passage describes the differences between pure and impure substances. Some words are missing. Insert the correct words from the list below into the spaces provided.

compound   **element**   **solid**   **impure**   **pure**

In chemistry, a _____ substance means that it only contains one type of atom or type of compound. An _____ substance contains more than one type of atom or compound mixed together. A substance which is made up of one type of atom is called an _____ whereas a _____ has more than one type of atom chemically joined together. [4]

2 Lisa is carrying out a distillation to separate the chemicals in a perfume that make up the scent. She uses the apparatus in the diagram below.

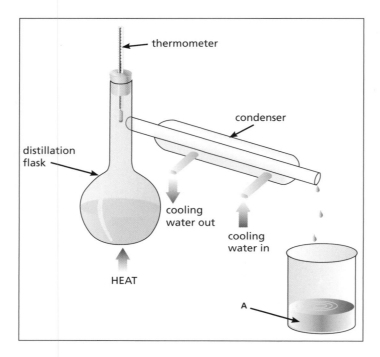

a) Which one of the following processes takes place during the experiment?

Tick (✓) the correct box.

Condensing then solidifying ☐   Condensing then evaporating ☐

Melting then boiling ☐   Evaporating then condensing ☐

Evaporating then melting ☐

[1]

b) Water enters the apparatus at 10 °C. The water will be a different temperature when it leaves the apparatus.

How would the temperature change? Explain the reason for your answer.

....

.... [2]

c) What is the scientific name for the liquid collected at the end of the experiment (substance **A**)?

.... [1]

3 Write the **word equation** for combustion of a hydrocarbon-based fuel in the space below.

.... + ... ➔ .... + ... [2]

4 Look at the diagrams below. Each shows a specific reaction.

A carbon + oxygen → carbon dioxide

B calcium carbonate → calcium oxide + carbon dioxide

C fuel + oxygen → carbon dioxide + water + energy

a) Which of the reactions shows **thermal decomposition**? .... [1]

b) Which two of the reactions give out heat? .... and .... [1]

c) How do we know that mass is conserved in each of these reactions?

....

.... [2]

Total Marks .... / 14

Chemistry

Elements, Compounds and Reactions

1 The following table lists a number of different chemicals.

Write whether they are an **element**, **mixture** or **compound** in the space provided.

Name of substance	Type of substance
Distilled water	
Gold	
Glucose	
Salt water	

[4]

2 The atomic number for the element carbon is 6.

What is the atomic number for the following elements?

a) vanadium = ...   **b)** copper = ...   **c)** sulfur = ...   **d)** oxygen = ...   [4]

3 Donna is conducting an experiment to investigate the reactions of metals.

The diagram shows the reaction of some metals in group 2 of the periodic table.

a) In tube C draw what would happen if calcium was added.

b) In each reaction a gas was produced. When a lit splint was added to the mouth of the test tube it made a squeaky-pop sound.

What is the name of the gas produced?

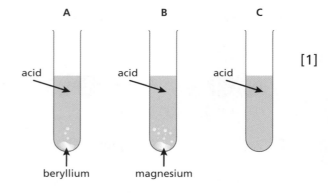

.... [1]

c) Each metal reacted with the acid. How do we know a chemical reaction took place?

....

.... [2]

[1]

4 A chemical catalogue lists glucose along with its chemical formula, $C_6H_{12}O_6$.

What is the total number of **atoms** present in a single molecule of glucose?

.... atoms   [1]

5 The following objects have been made out of a metal.

Each metal has a property that makes it especially useful for the object's role.

Draw a single line to connect each object to the correct property.

Copper saucepan

Wedding ring

Lightning conductor

Church bell

Sonorous

Conducts heat

Shiny

Conducts electricity

[3]

6 a) Look at the following chemical reactions and tick (✓) the correct boxes to show the **two** reactions that are written correctly.

　　i) magnesium + sulfuric acid ➜ magnesium nitrate + hydrogen ☐

　　ii) copper oxide + hydrochloric acid ➜ copper chloride + water ☐

　　iii) iron + phosphoric acid ➜ iron phosphate + hydrogen ☐

　　iv) lithium oxide + nitric acid ➜ lithium nitrate + hydrogen ☐

[2]

b) What is the name given to the process whereby oxygen is added to an atom?

_____ [1]

c) Magnesium can be burned in air, producing a bright white light and a white, powdery residue.

Write the chemical formula for the **product** in the space below.

_____ [2]

Total Marks _____ / 21

Chemistry

Explaining Physical Changes

1 For atoms to increase in temperature, what energy must they possess?

Tick (✓) the correct box.

Atomic energy ☐   Kinetic energy ☐

Heat energy ☐   Chemical energy ☐   [1]

2 Sally is testing a CO_2 fire extinguisher. The gas is stored inside the extinguisher until a valve is open.

a) Draw the arrangement of CO_2 molecules inside the extinguisher.

[1]

b) Sally places a handkerchief over the nozzle of the fire extinguisher, and then sets the extinguisher off. This causes some of the CO_2 to be collected in the handkerchief as solid dry ice.

Draw the arrangement of particles in the solid dry ice in the box below.

[1]

c) What is the name given to the process of a substance turning directly from a solid to a gas?

_____   [1]

3 The North Pole is situated on a floating mass of ice. Antarctica is a continent covered in ice.

Suggest why global warming will be a more severe problem if the ice in Antarctica melts compared to the ice at the North Pole melting.

[3]

4 In the 19th Century, Robert Brown observed pollen grains suspended in water, apparently moving of their own accord. This motion came to be called 'Brownian motion'.

a) The diagram shows the view through a microscope of a single pollen grain. Draw arrows on the diagram to show the Brownian motion of the pollen grain that you would see over a short period of time.

[1]

b) Describe what would happen to the Brownian motion of the pollen grain if the water it was in were heated.

[1]

c) Explain why this would be the case.

[3]

5 A cinema chain is considering introducing Smell-o-Vision. During the film, certain smells are sprayed from the back of the cinema to fit with the scene of the movie that is showing.

a) Explain, using the concept of diffusion, why this will not be effective for movies.

[3]

b) A scientist suggests having nozzles attached to every seat in the cinema.

Suggest why this would be better than the original idea.

[2]

Total Marks _____ / 17

Chemistry

1 Look at the following diagrams showing different chemical reactions. Each reaction is **incomplete**. Using the chemical equations provided, add molecules and / or atoms to correctly balance the reaction.

a) O_2 (g) + $2H_2$ (g) ⟶ $2H_2O$ (l) [2]

b) Cl_2 (g) + H_2 (g) ⟶ $2HCl$ (aq) [2]

2 Which of the following statements about catalysts is **true**?

Tick (✓) the correct box.

Metals cannot be catalysts. ☐

Catalysts have to be replaced regularly. ☐

Catalysts are a reactant in a reaction. ☐

Catalysts are not used up in a reaction. ☐ [1]

3 a) Write the **word equation** for the combustion of methane in air.

_____ + _____ → _____ + _____ [2]

b) Methane has the chemical formula CH_4. Write the **chemical equation** for the reaction of methane in oxygen.

_____ + _____ → _____ + _____ [2]

4 Kala is stung by a bee.

The bee's sting is acidic.

a) What substance is the chemical opposite of an acid?

.... [1]

b) Which of the following might be able to neutralise the acidic bee sting?

Tick (✓) the correct answer.

Vinegar ☐   Water ☐

Baking soda ☐   Copper ☐

[1]

5 Complete the following chemical reactions.

a) acid + ... ➔ salt + water [1]

b) .... + metal hydroxide ➔ salt + water [1]

c) acid + metal carbonate ➔ .... + water + ... [2]

6 Doris planted some hydrangeas in her garden. Hydrangeas change colour depending upon the pH of the soil: blue in low pH soil and pink in high pH soil.

She planted two sets of plants and was surprised to see that when they flowered one set had blue flowers and the other pink.

She wants all the flowers in her garden to be blue, not pink.

Suggest what she needs to do to ensure all her flowers are blue.

....

....

....

.... [2]

Total Marks .... / 17

Chemistry

Obtaining Useful Materials

1 Gold and silver are among a group of metals that are found in their elemental form on the Earth.

a) Explain why these metals are found in their elemental form.

_____ [1]

b) Suggest why metals such as iron were discovered much later in human history than gold and silver.

_____

_____ [2]

2 The material polythene is a polymer. Which of the following words means the unit that, when chemically joined together, makes a polymer?

Tick (✓) the correct answer.

Mono atomic ☐

Dimer ☐

Monomer ☐

Diatomic ☐   [1]

3 Materials can be classed into different categories. Match each material to its correct category using a single line.

Material	Category
Chained molecules made of repeating units	Polymer
A non-metallic material heated to high temperatures then cooled	Composite
A material made of more than one type of material chemically bonded together	Ceramic

[3]

4 Michael and Jeremy are carrying out an investigation. They place pieces of metals into tubes and observe what happens.

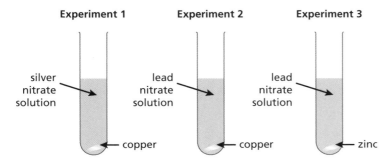

Experiment 1   Experiment 2   Experiment 3

silver nitrate solution → copper

lead nitrate solution → copper

lead nitrate solution → zinc

Michael observed that there were crystals of silver on the copper wire in experiment 1 and crystals of lead on the zinc wire in experiment 3 but no change in experiment 2.

a) From Michael's observations, write the order of reactivity of the four metals, copper, lead, silver and zinc.

....

   Most reactive   Least reactive   [2]

b) Jeremy took new pieces of each metal and added it to dilute sulfuric acid.
One of the metals reacted, the others stayed the same.

Suggest which metal reacted.

....   [1]

c) The boys decided to predict what would happen if a piece of zinc was added to silver nitrate solution.

Suggest who is correct and explain why.

I don't think that the zinc will react

I think the zinc will react

Michael   Jeremy

.... because ....

....

....   [2]

5 Suggest why helicopter rotor blades are made of carbon fibre rather than wood.

....

....

....   [3]

Total Marks .... / 15

Chemistry

Using our Earth Sustainably

1 Add labels to the diagram of the structure of the Earth. Choose from the list below.

crust   **inner mantle**   **core**   **mantle**

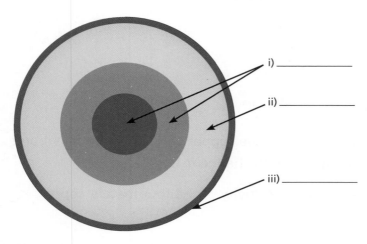

i) _____

ii) _____

iii) _____

[2]

2 Look at the diagrams of two igneous rock samples.

Rock A (Small crystals)

Rock B (Large crystals)

a) Suggest why the crystals are different sizes in both igneous rocks.

_____

_____

_____ [2]

b) What is the name for the type of rock which involves the rock being weathered and eroded, transported and settling?

Tick (✓) the correct answer.

Metamorphic ☐

Igneous ☐

Sedimentary ☐

Diatomaceous ☐

[1]

3 Complete the table showing how the percentages of gases in the Earth's atmosphere vary. Choose from the names provided below.

carbon dioxide   **oxygen**   **nitrogen**

Gas	Percentage in Atmosphere
	78
	21
	0.04

[3]

4 The carbon cycle shows the movement of carbon atoms.

a) Which letter indicates carbon that is effectively locked in for millions of years?

....

[1]

b) Which letter indicates the removal of carbon from the atmosphere?

....

[1]

c) Governments around the world are trying to reduce man-made carbon dioxide emissions.

What is the reason for this?

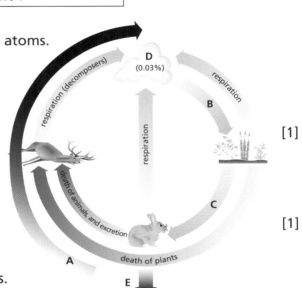

....

....

[2]

5 Read the following newspaper article.

Rare earth metals getting rarer by the minute

Modern smartphones use elements such as yttrium and dysprosium. These metals are rare because mining is extremely complex and expensive as well as being harmful for the environment. In recent years countries such as China have restricted the export of the so called rare earth metals.

What can we do to ensure that the rare earth metals so important to modern technology are not lost forever?

....

....

[2]

Total Marks .... / 14

Physics

Forces and their Effects

1 Natasha is playing tennis. She throws the ball in the air to serve then hits it with her racket.

The diagram below shows the point at which she hits the ball with the racket.

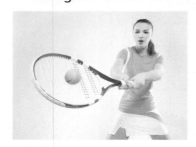

a) Draw and label **two** arrows on the ball to show the forces acting on the ball. [2]

b) What **type** of force is the racket applying to the ball?

Tick (✓) the correct answer.

Fast ☐   Push ☐

Pull ☐   Twist ☐ [1]

2 Roger is measuring the weights of four different objects.

He uses a Newton meter to determine the weight.

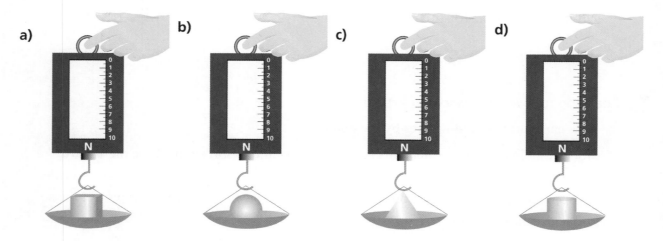

Object A weighs 8.0 N, B weighs 2.3 N, C weighs 6.4 N and D weighs 0.2 N

a) On the diagram for each Newton meter, draw a line to show the weight measured. [4]

b) Roger now wants to measure the weight of an object that is over 15 N. What will he have to do to measure the object's weight?

.... [1]

3 Penny is measuring the speeds of a toy car being pushed down a ramp. She changes the angle of the ramp each time and measures the time taken to pass a marker on the table.

Penny records her results in a table.

Angle of ramp (°)	Distance to marker (cm)	Time taken (s)	Speed (cm/s)
10	30	2.5	12.0
20	30		15.7
30	30	1.2	
40	30		33.3
50	30	0.8	37.5

Some results are missing in the table. Add the missing data. [3]

4 A spring is stretched and the results recorded in a table.

Weight (N)	Stretch of spring (cm)
100	2
200	4
300	5
400	9
500	10

a) Plot the points on the graph and draw a line of best fit.

[2]

b) Explain Hooke's Law and suggest why the spring obeys Hooke's Law.

....

....

.... [2]

Total Marks .... / 15

Physics

Exploring Contact and Non-Contact Forces

1. Farah has been given a 'Floating Globe'.

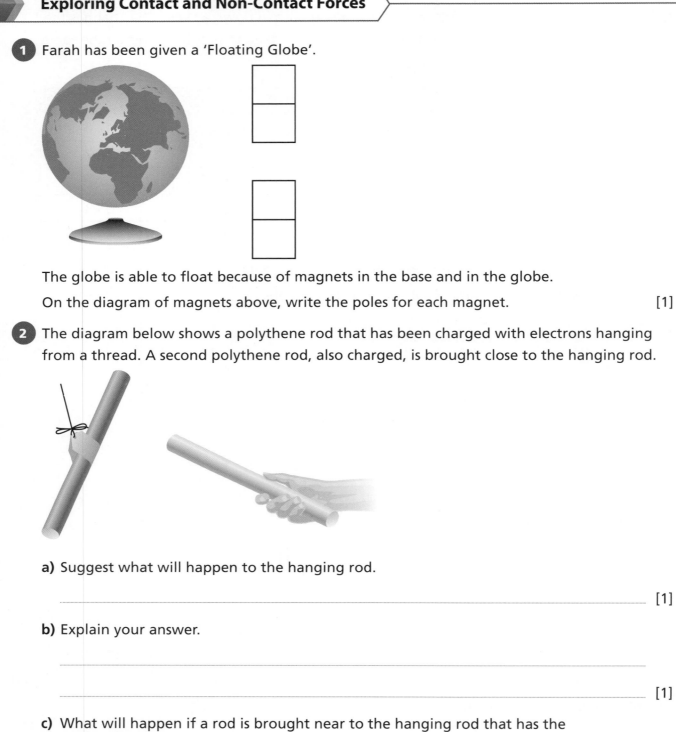

   The globe is able to float because of magnets in the base and in the globe.

   On the diagram of magnets above, write the poles for each magnet. [1]

2. The diagram below shows a polythene rod that has been charged with electrons hanging from a thread. A second polythene rod, also charged, is brought close to the hanging rod.

   a) Suggest what will happen to the hanging rod.

   .... [1]

   b) Explain your answer.

   ....

   .... [1]

   c) What will happen if a rod is brought near to the hanging rod that has the opposite charge?

   .... [1]

3 Animals are adapted to the habitats they live in.

a) A gerbil is adapted to living in the sandy desert. Suggest how its feet are adapted for living in the desert.

....

....

.... [2]

b) A polar bear is adapted to living in the arctic.

If the polar bear has a weight of 4500 N and each paw has an area of 2400 cm², calculate the pressure of the polar bear on the snow. Show your working out.

....

....

.... [3]

4 A boat travels from the river Thames into the English Channel. Which of the following statements are correct? Tick (✓) **two** correct boxes.

There will be the same amount of water displaced in the Thames compared to the Channel. ☐

There will be more water displaced in the Channel as there is more available. ☐

There will be less water displaced in the Channel as there is more upthrust. ☐

Fresh water contains less dissolved salts, so upthrust will be lower. ☐

[2]

Total Marks .... / 11

Physics

1 A spring has a 200 N weight attached.

What is the reaction force from the spring?

_____ [1]

2 Sheldon monitored how his cat moved over an 11 minute period. Use the distance–time graph to answer the following questions.

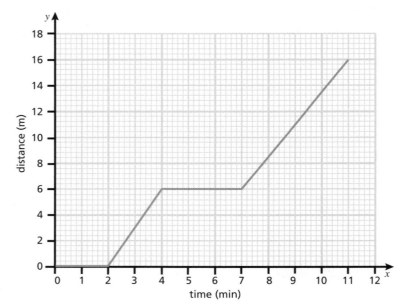

a) The description of the cat's journey has been shuffled. Sort the statements into the correct order.

A   The cat moved 10 m over 4 min at a constant speed.

B   The cat stopped for 2 min.

C   The cat moved 6 m over 2 min at a constant speed.

D   The cat stopped for 3 min.

_____ _____ _____ _____ [1]

b) What is the cat's average speed over the 11 minutes? Show your working.

_____

_____ [2]

3 Arran is sitting on a train travelling at 120 km/h. Another train is on the next track travelling in the same direction at 120 km/h. Arran can see Triston standing in the next train.

a) To Arran, how fast does Triston appear to be travelling?

_____ [1]

b) The trains pass a station. How fast does the station appear to be travelling to Triston?

_____ [1]

4 The planets in our solar system are all in orbit around our closest star, the Sun.

a) What force keeps the planets in orbit around the Sun?

.... [1]

b) It is possible that in another part of the galaxy there is a star with eight planets in orbit around it.

If the star had twice the mass of the Sun, how will the mass of the star affect the orbit of the planets around it?

.... [1]

5 Look at the diagram of the Earth orbiting the Sun.

a) Add the labels below to the diagram.

21st December   **21st June**   **21st March**   **21st September**   [2]

b) Read the following statements. One of the statements is false.
Put a cross (✗) alongside it.

On 21st March the length of day and night are the same. ☐

The Earth is tilted with respect to the North Star. ☐

In the Northern Hemisphere during winter, day length gets progressively longer. ☐

In the Southern Hemisphere during summer, day length gets progressively longer. ☐ [1]

6 The gravitational field strength of Mars is 3.72 N/kg.

a) If an astronaut with a mass of 80 kg were to land on Mars, what would her weight be?

.... [1]

b) What would her weight be on Earth?

.... [1]

Total Marks .... / 13

Physics

1 Syra dives into a swimming pool. The diagram shows different positions as she dives.

a) Which of the diagrams shows the point where Syra has the most gravitational potential energy?

.... [1]

b) At what point does Syra have the greatest kinetic energy?

.... [1]

c) Syra's kinetic energy was 300 J at point C. What was her gravitational potential energy at point A? Tick (✓) the correct answer.

0 J ☐   300 J ☐

150 J ☐   600 J ☐   [1]

2 Mustafa is investigating the amount of energy stored in different foods.

He sets up the equipment as shown in the diagram.

Food	Temperature change (°C)
Peanut	25
Cream cracker	28
Walnut	19

a) Which food contained the **most** energy?

.... [1]

b) Write the word equation for combustion in the space below.

.... [1]

c) Name the energy changes that occur when burning a peanut.

.... [3]

3 When you are standing at a railway station an approaching train can be heard through the railway line before the train can be heard through the air.

Explain why sound travels faster in a railway line compared to through the air.

....

....

.... **[3]**

4 Look at the ultrasound photograph.

Ultrasound is used to see the developing baby inside the womb.

Which of the following properties are reasons why ultrasound is used to see developing babies? Tick (✓) the **two** correct answers.

Ultrasound has a frequency higher than 20,000 Hz. ☐

Ultrasound waves cannot be reflected. ☐

Ultrasound can displace dirt from objects. ☐

Ultrasound does not harm the baby. ☐ **[2]**

5 A spy agency manages to listen in to a conversation between two suspects in a room. They shine a laser at the suspects' window and reflect it onto a detector. The movement of the glass in the window pane changes. This leads to differences in the laser reflection that can then be decoded and converted into sound.

a) What causes the windows to vibrate in the first place?

.... **[1]**

b) This technique only works in a small room. Suggest why it would not work as well if the suspects were in a hall, for example.

....

.... **[2]**

Total Marks .... / 16

Physics

1. Naveen has set up four circuits.

A   B

C 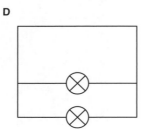 D

a) Which circuit will work? .... [1]

b) Naveen has a personal alarm. It has a speaker that sounds when the emergency switch is pressed.

The diagrams below show the symbols for a battery, a loudspeaker and a switch.

In the space below, draw a series circuit diagram for the alarm using these symbols.

[1]

c) Which part of the circuit provides the energy for the circuit?

.... [1]

2 Ges is an electrician. He has been taking measurements of voltage, current and resistance. He has recorded them in the table below.

Voltage (V)	Current (A)	Resistance (Ω)
2	0.5	
6		3
	2	4

a) Ges has missed out some data in his table. Add the missing data. Remember that resistance = $\frac{\text{voltage}}{\text{current}}$. [3]

b) What is meant by the electrical term, **resistance**?

[1]

3 Lisa tests an electromagnet. She uses ball-bearings to test the strength of the electromagnet.

a) What effect does increasing the number of coils have on an electromagnet?

[1]

b) Name **two** other ways of achieving the same effect described in 3a).

[2]

c) When Lisa switches off the electromagnets she notices that the ball-bearings fall from the iron core but stay attached to the steel core.

Suggest which core would be best for an electromagnet. Explain your answer.

[2]

4 Explain why navigation compasses point North on Earth.

[3]

Total Marks _____ / 15

Physics

1 Quetzal is investigating waves using a ripple tank.

The diagrams show the different waves he observed during the experiment.

A

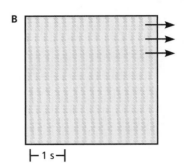

B

a) What is the **frequency** in Hz of each of the four observed waves?

A ....

B ....

C ....

D ....

C

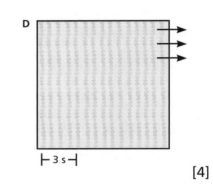

D

[4]

b) Quetzal then draws a wave with a frequency of 1 Hz. Add labels to the wave using the words provided.

amplitude **peak** **trough** **wavelength**

[2]

2 Noise cancelling headphones contain microphones that record external noise and then play it back to the listener. The sound played is out of phase with the external noise.

Explain how the waves cancel, using diagrams of waves in your answer.

....

....

....

....

....

....

[4]

3 Isabella shines a light on a piece of paper and a mirror.

a) **In the space below**, draw what happens to the light for each case. Use **four** light rays for each example.

      Paper   **Mirror**   [3]

b) Isabella next uses a laser and shines it at the mirror. This time she measures the angle of incidence and the angle of reflection.

Complete the table to show Isabella's experimental results.

Experiment	Angle of incidence (°)	Angle of reflection (°)
1	25	
2		60
3	90	

[3]

c) Which of Isabella's experiments represents a 'normal' ray of light?

    ....

[1]

4 Sara is taking Phil's photograph using a pinhole camera.

a) Draw the ray of light from Phil's head and feet and show how the light enters the pinhole camera.

[2]

Phil

screen

pinhole camera

b) Sara has another camera. It has a lens.

On the diagram, show the passage of light through the lens.

Indicate the focal point.

[3]

Total Marks .... / 22

Mixed Test-Style Questions

1 Peter is an athlete in the Olympics.

Peter is standing on the track, about to start the race.

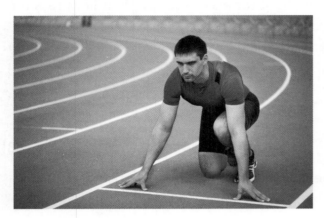

a) **On the diagram above,** draw and label **two** arrows to show the **two** forces acting on Peter when he is stationary before the race.

2 marks

b) Peter's mass is 70 kg. What is his weight?

_____ N

1 mark

c) Peter runs in the 1600 m event.

His time for the race is 5 min 30 s.

What was his average speed for the race? Show your working out.

_____

_____

_____

2 marks

d) Peter's trainer suggests that Peter needs to run the next qualifying race at an average speed of 5.3 m/s.

How long would it take for Peter to cross the finish line if he succeeds in running at that speed?

_____

_____

_____

2 marks

e) i) Peter returns to the Olympic Village after the race.

In his room a book is sitting on a table.

Its mass is 180 g.

What will be the reaction force from the table?

Tick (✓) the correct box.

180 N ☐

18 N ☐

1.8 N ☐

0.18 N ☐

1 mark

ii) The following table lists the gravitational field strength on three other planets.

Planet	Gravitational Field Strength (N/kg)
Mars	3.7
Jupiter	25
Neptune	12

What would be the weight of Peter's book on Mars and Neptune?

Mars _____ N

Neptune _____ N

1 mark

iii) What would **Peter's** weight be on Jupiter?

_____ N

1 mark

f) Which of the following is the cause of the gravitational field strength of a planet?

Tick (✓) the correct box.

Size ☐

Colour ☐

Distance from Sun ☐

Mass ☐

1 mark

TOTAL ☐

11

Mixed Test-Style Questions

2 This question is about cells.

a) Look at the list of cell parts.

Some are found in plant cells. Some are found in animal cells.

Some are found in both animal and plant cells.

Write each word in the appropriate column of the table below to show where it is found (note that some of them will appear in both columns).

cell wall   chloroplast   cytoplasm   membrane   mitochondria   nucleus   vacuole

Plant Cell	Animal cell

7 marks

b) These statements are about unicellular and multicellular organisms.

Write a **U** in the boxes next to the statements about unicellular organisms.

Write an **M** in the boxes next to the statements about multicellular organisms.

Made of lots of cells	
Cells perform many different jobs	
Each cell depends upon many other cells	
Cells are specialised	
Made of just one cell	

5 marks

c) Put the following words in their correct order to show levels of organisation, from smallest to largest.

The first has been done for you.

cell   organ   organism   system   tissue

cell   _____   _____   _____

3 marks

d) Most body cells in human beings contain 46 chromosomes.

The diagram shows how genetic information is inherited from our parents.

Complete the diagram to show how many chromosomes are in each cell.

Body cell from mum and dad

Sperm and ova cells

Fertilised cell

5 marks

e) Each body cell contains all the information needed to make a new human being.

Draw straight lines to join each **part** of a cell with its correct **function**.

Part	Function
Nucleus	A single instruction for making one protein
Chromosome	Part of the cell that contains the chromosomes
Gene	A length of DNA that consists of many different genes

3 marks

f) Substances move between cells by diffusion.

i) Explain what is meant by diffusion and how it works.

....

....

....

3 marks

ii) Write down two examples of diffusion that occur in humans.

1. ....

2. ....

2 marks

TOTAL

28

3 The following images show some different objects in Nicki's garden. Each object is made of a different material.

Plastic garden gnome

Aluminium and glass greenhouse

Concrete bird bath

Plastic playhouse

Steel watering can

Copper weather vane

a) i) Which of the objects are made of a **polymer**?

1. _____

2. _____

2 marks

ii) Which of the objects is made of an **element**?

_____

1 mark

iii) Which object is made of **composite**?

_____

1 mark

b) Iron **rusts**.

Write the **word equation** for rusting in the space below.

_____ + _____ + _____ → _____

2 marks

c) A friend gives Nicki another garden gnome.
This one is made of iron.

Suggest what Nicki can do to stop it rusting and explain how your suggestion would work.

....

....

....

d) Which of the following are **not** properties of iron?

Tick (✓) the **three** correct answers.

Low melting point	
Gas at room temperature	
Malleable	
Sonorous	
Low density	
Conducts heat	

2 marks

e) Nicki works at a sports car manufacturer. The sports car traditionally made at the factory had plastic bodywork.

Nicki suggests that the newest car model could be made out of carbon fibre.

i) What type of material is carbon fibre?

....

1 marks

ii) Carbon fibre is very expensive.

Give two reasons why Nicki suggested the body of the car could be made out of carbon fibre.

....

....

2 marks

TOTAL

13

Mixed Test-Style Questions

4 There are two types of respiration: **aerobic** respiration and **anaerobic** respiration.

a) The following words all refer to respiration.

Some are concerned with aerobic respiration, some are concerned with anaerobic respiration and some with both.

Write each word in the appropriate diagram. You can use the words more than once.

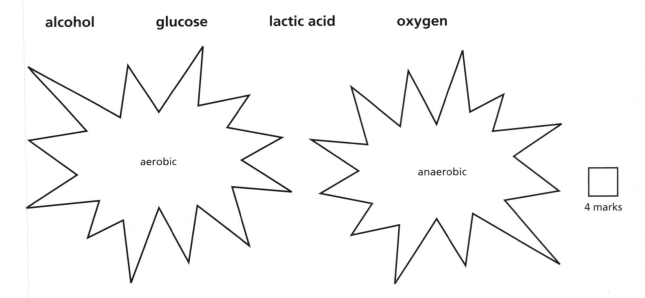

alcohol   glucose   lactic acid   oxygen

aerobic

anaerobic

4 marks

b) Anaerobic respiration in humans is different to anaerobic respiration in yeast.

Put a tick (✓) in the box next to the **two** correct differences between anaerobic respiration in humans and yeast.

During anaerobic respiration…

glucose is used in humans but not in yeast	
lactic acid is produced in humans but not in yeast	
carbon dioxide is produced in yeast but not in humans	
alcohol is produced in humans but not in yeast	
energy is released in humans but not in yeast	

2 marks

c) Anaerobic respiration in humans releases less energy than aerobic respiration.

Suggest why humans use anaerobic respiration even though it releases less energy.

_____

_____

1 mark

d) Respiration provides energy for muscles to work. Muscles exert a force to move a joint.

Look at the diagram.

Calculate the force required by the muscle to raise the lower arm.

Show your working out.

10 kg weight — muscle — upper arm

30 cm |5 cm

3 marks

e) In order to get enough energy, a young man needs to eat food containing 2500 kcal each day.

Explain what will happen if he eats 3000 kcal each day.

2 marks

f) Energy in food can be measured in calories or Joules.

1 kcal = 4.2 kJ

How many kJ are contained in 2500 kcal?

Show your working out.

2 marks

g) Respiration also occurs in green plants.

Suggest why green plants need to respire even though they obtain energy from sunlight during photosynthesis.

2 marks

TOTAL

16

5 Mark is investigating a claim that an orange coloured sweet contains illegal food colouring.

He decides to use chromatography to check the colours of the sweet.

He places a sample of the sweet along with the E-number dyes which are for the legal food colourings onto chromatography paper.

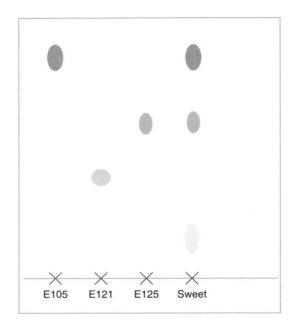

a) Explain why the samples of food colouring are placed on a pencil-drawn line.

_____

_____

1 mark

b) The different food colours move different distances.

Which of the following is the **best** explanation for this?

Tick (✓) the correct box.

Colours have different wavelengths.

The least soluble colourings travel the furthest.

The most soluble colourings travel the furthest.

The longer the colouring, the further it will travel.

1 mark

c) Which of the colours does **not** appear in the chromatogram for the sweet?

_____

1 mark

d) On the chromatogram, for sample X draw what would be seen if sample X contained E105 and E121? Draw your answer on the chromatogram below.

2 marks

e) E125 is a red dye that is only permitted for externally applied drugs and cosmetics in the USA.

Suggest whether the sweet Mark is investigating is fit for people to eat.

Explain how you reached your conclusion.

2 marks

f) Mark makes a second chromatogram, this time using different colour permanent markers. To his surprise none of the dots move up the chromatogram.

Suggest why the permanent marker dots did not move up the chromatogram.

1 mark

TOTAL

8

6 Astra shines a white light through a glass prism.

On the screen she sees a spectrum.

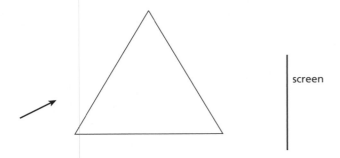

screen

a) **Draw the ray of light** as it passes through the prism and then onto the screen.

2 marks

b) Which of the colours in the spectrum is refracted the **least**?

Tick (✓) the correct box.

Red ☐

Yellow ☐

Blue ☐

Violet ☐

1 mark

c) In the human eye, what colour light do the three colour-detecting cone cells absorb?

_____

_____

1 mark

d) Astra takes a torch and shines it onto a mirror.

The mirror reflects the light.

i) She shines the light at a 45° angle.

Complete the diagram to show the **incident** and **reflected** rays.

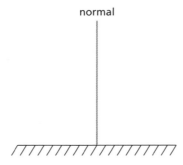

normal

2 marks

ii) State the **law of reflection**.

....

....

....

1 mark

e) A pinhole camera is able to form an image at the back of the camera.

The image is always upside down.

pinhole camera

Explain why the image is **upside down**.

....

....

....

....

....

....

2 marks

TOTAL

9

7 Naomi is experimenting with metals. She adds a piece of a different metal to each test tube.

She added 3 cm³ of sulfuric acid to each tube.

The diagram below shows her results.

a) Naomi realises some of the metals are reacting with the acid.

Suggest how Naomi knows this.

....

....

1 mark

b) Complete the table to show the names of the salts formed in this experiment.

Metal	Salt
Copper	Copper sulfate
Tin	
Iron	
Magnesium	

1 mark

c) Write the order of reactivity of the four metals, starting with the least reactive and going to the most reactive.

Least reactive ....

....

....

Most reactive ....

1 mark

d) Predict what would happen if Naomi were to set up another tube, this time with calcium and sulfuric acid.

Draw what you would expect to see.

1 mark

e) Naomi takes a piece of iron and adds it to a solution of iron sulfate.

Predict what will happen. Explain your answer.

....

....

....

1 mark

f) Write down the chemical equation for the reaction between calcium and sulfuric acid.

Show the state symbols.

.... + ... ⟶ .... + ...

3 marks

TOTAL

8

Mixed Test-Style Questions

8 This question is about interdependence.

a) Interdependence can be shown in food chains.

Look at this food chain.

crop   moths   dormice   foxes

A farmer sprays his crop with insecticide.

The numbers below show the relative amounts of insecticide found in organisms in a food chain.

Write each number underneath the correct organism in the food chain.

1 10 100 1000

4 marks

b) Which of these statements about the interdependence of plants and animals are true?

Put a tick (✓) next to the **three** correct answers.

Plants provide animals with food. ☐

Animals provide plants with carbon dioxide. ☐

Plants provide animals with carbon dioxide. ☐

Animals provide plants with energy. ☐

Animals provide plants with oxygen. ☐

Plants provide animals with oxygen. ☐

3 marks

c) The energy for food webs is provided by photosynthesis in plants' leaves.

Leaves are adapted to do the job of photosynthesis.

Draw straight lines to join each leaf **adaptation** to its correct **explanation**.

Adaptation	Explanation
Large surface area	Contain chlorophyll for photosynthesis
Small holes on the underside of the leaf	To allow carbon dioxide into the leaf and oxygen to leave the leaf
Are green in colour	To collect as much sunlight energy as possible

2 marks

d) Look at the word equation for photosynthesis.

The equation contains **two mistakes**.

Draw a (ring) around each mistake.

light

water + oxygen   ⟶   glucose + carbon dioxide + energy

chlorophyll

2 marks

e) Variation and biodiversity are important to maintain a food web.

Which of these statements about variation are true?

Put a tick (✓) in the box next to the **two** correct answers.

Variation is a list of all the similarities in a group of organisms.

Variation increases when biodiversity decreases.

Variation can be continuous or discontinuous.

Variation increases the risk of extinction.

Variation increases the chance of survival when an environment changes.

2 marks

f) Look at the diagram of the food web.

Add the following food chain to the food web.

grass ⟶ moths ⟶ blue tits ⟶ foxes

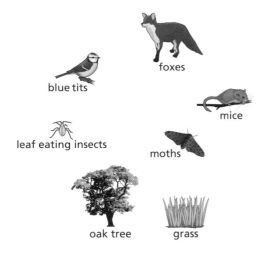

foxes

blue tits

mice

leaf eating insects

moths

oak tree   grass

3 marks

TOTAL

16

Notes

Answers

Page 148–149 Cells – the Building Blocks of Life

1. **a)** animal cell; **i)** cytoplasm, **ii)** nucleus, **iii)** cell membrane **[4]**
   b) plant cell; **i)** cell wall, **ii)** cytoplasm, **iii)** nucleus, **iv)** chloroplast, **v)** vacuole, **vi)** membrane **[7]**

2. Oxygen and carbon dioxide move in and out of cells by diffusion. **[1]**

3.

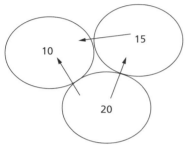

   [all correct **2** marks, **0** marks for 1 correct]

4.

Job	Part of cell	Found in...
Makes food from light energy	Chloroplast	Plant
Supports the cell	Cell wall	Plant
Controls what enters and leaves the cell	Cell membrane	Both
Where chemical reactions take place	Cytoplasm	Both
Provides support to the cell	Vacuole	Plant

   [need both part of cell and where found for **[1]** each, total of **5** marks]

5. *Answers may vary but could include*: muscle cell moves skeleton **[1]**; nerve cell carries electrical impulses **[1]**; red blood cell carries oxygen **[1]**.

6. fertilisation; gestation; birth **[3]**
7. pollinated by wind **[1]**

Pages 150–151 Eating, Drinking and Breathing

1. diaphragm – muscles that contract to breathe in; bronchioles – tubes that carry air in and out of the lungs; alveoli – small air sacs where gas exchange takes place; intercostal muscles – muscles that raise and lower the ribs [**3** marks for all correct, **2** marks for 3 correct, **1** mark for 2 correct, **none** for 1 correct]

2. when the lungs increase in volume the pressure drops **[1]**; oxygen diffuses from the alveoli into the blood **[1]**

   Just learn the steps for breathing in. Then reverse the steps for breathing out.

3. Asthma causes the airways to narrow. **[1]**
4. Carbohydrates and fats – gives our body energy; protein – used for growth and new tissue; vitamins – used to help chemical reactions take place; minerals – needed for strong bones and teeth; water – dissolves chemicals so that chemical reactions can take place [**4** marks for all correct, **3** for 3 correct, **1** for 2 correct, none for 1 correct]

   Try to make sure connecting lines are drawn using a ruler.

5. oesophagus before stomach **[1]**; stomach before small intestine **[1]**; small intestine before large intestine **[1]**; large intestine before rectum **[1]**; rectum before anus **[1]**

   Write your answers in pencil first. Then you can rub them out and correct them if you want to change the order.

6. The large intestine is where water is absorbed; the pancreas produces enzymes to help digest food; the small intestine is where most food is broken down chemically. **[3]**

Pages 152–153 Getting the Energy your Body Needs

1. releasing energy from food **[1]**
2. glucose → lactic acid + energy **[3]**

   > If a question asks for a word equation, never write down the chemical equation as you are more likely to make a mistake.

3. aerobic – releases the most energy **[1]** and uses oxygen **[1]**; anaerobic – produces lactic acid **[1]** and produces alcohol **[1]**

   > Remember, aerobic uses air containing oxygen.

4. sunlight **[1]**
5. not done: digests food **[1]**; transports nerve impulses around the body **[1]**; pumps blood around the body **[1]**

   > This question does not say how many crosses to use. The clue is in the number of marks awarded.

6. i) bone; ii) bone; iii) cartilage; iv) fluid; v) ligament **[5]**

   > Only use the words provided by the question.

7. Muscles can only contract, they cannot push **[1]**. So in order to move a joint they have to work as an antagonistic pair **[1]** where one muscle pulls one way, one pulls the opposite way *or* where one muscle contracts the other relaxes **[1]**.

   > The number of marks tells you how many things you need to write.

Pages 154–155 Looking at Plants and Ecosystems

1.

light
water + carbon dioxide → glucose + oxygen
chlorophyll

water and carbon dioxide can be either way round, glucose and oxygen can be either way round

[1 mark for left-hand side of equation correct, 1 mark for right-hand side of equation correct, 1 mark for light and chlorophyll correct]

> The equation for aerobic respiration is the reverse of the equation for photosynthesis.

2. i) upper epidermis; ii) chloroplasts; iii) stoma; iv) lower epidermis
   [3 marks for all correct, 2 marks for 3 correct, 1 mark for 2 correct]

   > Only use the words provided by the question.

3. leaves have a large surface area; chlorophyll is found in leaves; there are small holes on the underside of leaves **[3]**

   > Only use the number of ticks the question asks for.

4. animals use oxygen and produce carbon dioxide; plants use carbon dioxide and produce oxygen **[2]**

   > Only use the number of ticks the question asks for.

5. any two of:
   lettuce → rabbit → sparrowhawk;
   lettuce → slug → thrush → sparrowhawk
   lettuce → rabbit → fox **[2]**

   > A food chain must include every step from the bottom to the top of a food web.

6. energy **[1]**

   > Only use the number of ticks the question asks for.

Pages 156–157 Variation for Survival

1. C and F **[2]**
2. cell before nucleus **[1]**; nucleus before chromosome **[1]**; chromosome before gene **[1]**

3. chromosome – a strand of DNA made up of genes; gene – a length of DNA that is just one code for a protein; nucleus – found in a cell and contains all the chromosomes. [**2** marks for all correct]

> Try to make sure connecting lines are drawn using a ruler.

4. Watson and Crick – developed a theory for the structure of DNA; Maurice Wilkins – produced evidence to support Watson and Crick's theory; Rosalind Franklin – made X-ray images of DNA [**2** marks for all correct]

> Try to make sure connecting lines are drawn using a ruler.

5. continuous – height [**1**], weight [**1**] discontinuous – blood groups [**1**], ability to roll tongue [**1**].

> Continuous is where there is a range; discontinuous is where there are separate groups.

6. when the environment changes some members of the species will be more likely to survive; members of the species that survive will breed to produce more offspring [**2**]

> Only use the number of ticks the question asks for.

7. the range of variation in a species in a habitat, *or* the number of species in a habitat [**1**]

> Learning definitions of words is an easy way to score marks.

8. D [**1**]

Pages 158–159 Our Health and the Effects of Drugs

1. A substance that affects the body. [**1**]

> Only use the number of ticks the question asks for.

2. Unwanted symptoms caused by taking the drug. [**1**]
3. White blood cells can engulf microbes; White blood cells produce chemicals to kill microbes. [**2**]
4. Cigarettes contain **nicotine** [**1**] which **speeds up** [**1**] heart rate and **raises** [**1**] blood pressure.
5. Vaccines cause the production of memory cells; Vaccines contain dead disease-causing organisms. [**2**]
6. A drug used for pleasure. [**1**]
7. A drug that is used to treat an illness. [**1**]
8. *Answers will vary but may include:* For legalisation – pain relief or freedom of choice [**1**] Against legalisation – leads to harder drugs or serious side effects [**1**]
9. Drugs which make you feel awake and alert are called **stimulants** [**1**]. Some drugs can make people think they can see things that are not there. They are called **hallucinogens** [**1**]. An example of a depressant drug is **cannabis** [**1**].

> Make sure you clearly underline the correct answers.

Pages 160–171 **Chemistry**

Pages 160–161 Mixing, Dissolving and Separating

1. In chemistry, a **pure** [**1**] substance means that it only contains one type of atom or type of compound. An **impure** [**1**] substance contains more than one type of atom or compound mixed together. A substance which is made up of one type of atom is called an **element** [**1**] whereas a **compound** [**1**] has more than one type of atom chemically joined together.

2. a) evaporating then condensing **[1]**
    b) The temperature would be warmer **[1]**
       as the water has been heated by the
       gas as it condenses into liquid **[1]**. Also
       accept: temperature above 30 °C.
    c) distillate **[1]**
3. fuel + oxygen ➔ carbon dioxide + water **[2]**
    [**1** mark for correct reactants; **1** mark for
    correct products]
4. a) B **[1]**
    b) A and C **[1]**
    c) The number of atoms of each element is
       the same on either side of the reaction **[1]**.
       Bubbles are produced **[1]**.

**Pages 162–163 Elements, Compounds and
Reactions**

1.

Name of substance	Type of substance
Distilled water	Compound
Gold	Element
Glucose	Compound
Salt water	Mixture

[4]

2. a) 23; b) 29; c) 16; d) 8 **[4]**

> Always make use of the periodic table
> provided in tests. Don't rely on
> memory alone.

3. a) *diagram should show calcium and more*
       bubbles (at least 15) **[1]**
    b) hydrogen **[1]**
    c) We know a chemical reaction took place
       because a new product **[1]** was formed
       from the reactants **[1]**.
4. number of atoms = 24 **[1]**
5. copper saucepan – conducts heat
    wedding ring – shiny
    lightning conductor – conducts electricity
    church bell – sonorous [**3** marks for all
    correct, **2** marks for 2 correct, **none**
    for 1 correct]

6. a) ii and iii **[2]**
    b) oxidation **[1]**
    c) MgO(s) **[2]**

Pages 164–165 Explaining Physical Changes
1. kinetic energy **[1]**
2. a) *To ensure that you obtain the marks, your*
       diagram should show a minimum
       of 5 atoms in a random arrangement,
       atoms not touching. Accept diagram
       where there are 5 molecules of CO_2
       (each molecule must be drawn correctly).

[1]

    b) *Diagram showing at least three rows of*
       particles, all touching.

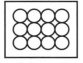

[1]
    c) sublimation **[1]**
3. The ice on Antarctica will cause the sea
    level to rise **[1]** because the ice is on land
    and not already floating in the sea **[1]**,
    unlike the ice at the North Pole which has
    already caused a sea level rise **[1]**.
4. a) *Diagram must show a random*
       zigzag pattern. **[1]**
    b) The grain would move faster. **[1]**
    c) The particles in the fluid surrounding
       the pollen grain **[1]** would acquire more
       kinetic energy **[1]** and so move and
       collide more frequently **[1]**.
5. a) The smells would diffuse **[1]** across
       the theatre randomly **[1]**. By the time
       everyone smelt the smell, the story
       would have moved on and the smell
       would no longer fit with what was on
       screen **[1]**.

b) The smells would not have far to travel [1]. This would mean that it would be more likely that the person watching the film would smell the smell at the appropriate point of the story [1].

Pages 166–167 Explaining Chemical Changes

1. a) [2]

 b) [2]

2. Catalysts are not used up in a reaction. [1]

3. a) methane + oxygen → carbon dioxide + water [2]
 [**1** mark for correct reactants; **1** mark for correct products]

 b) $CH_4(g) + 2O_2(g) → CO_2(g) + 2H_2O(l)$ [2]
 [**1** mark for correct reactants; **1** mark for correct products]

4. a) a base / alkali [1]

 b) Baking soda [1]

5. a) acid + **metal oxide/base** → salt + water [1]

 b) **acid** + metal hydroxide → salt + water [1]

 c) acid + metal carbonate → **salt** + water + **carbon dioxide** [2]

6. Doris needs to add acid or acidic fertilisers [1] to the soil to lower the pH so that the pH causes the flowers to be blue [1].

Pages 168–169 Obtaining Useful Materials

1. a) They are unreactive. [1]

 b) Humans had to discover ways to separate the metals [1] from their ores / oxygen [1].

2. monomer [1]

3. chained molecules made of repeating units – polymer; A non-metallic material heated to high temperatures then cooled – ceramic; A material made of more than one type of material chemically bonded together – composite [3]

4. a) zinc; lead; copper; silver
 [**2** marks all correct, **1** mark for three metals in correct positions, **0** marks for 2 correct]

b) zinc [1]

c) Jeremy because copper reacted with the silver nitrate and displaced the silver [1], and zinc is higher in the reactivity series than copper [1] .

The connective 'because' is extremely useful as it forces you to explain your answer. Practise using 'because' with all your answers.

5. Carbon fibre is a much lighter [1] and stronger [1] material than wood and so will be better able to tolerate the high stresses placed on it when the helicopter flies [1].

Pages 170–171 Using Our Earth Sustainably

1. i) core, ii) mantle, iii) crust [2]

2. a) In rock A the crystals are small. This indicates that the igneous rock cooled very rapidly [1]. Rock B shows much larger crystals. This means that the rock cooled over a longer period of time [1].

 b) sedimentary [1]

3.

Gas	Percentage in Atmosphere
Nitrogen	78
Oxygen	21
Carbon dioxide	0.04

[3]

4. a) E [1]

 b) B [1]

 c) Carbon dioxide is a greenhouse gas [1]. The more in our atmosphere, the higher the temperature will rise and this will cause climate change [1]. (The activities of man are creating more carbon dioxide than would be present naturally.)

5. Send items to a recycling centre to extract the rare earth metals so that they can be used again [1], rather than dumping in landfill [1].

Pages 172–173 Forces and their Effects

1. a)

force/weight of ball on racket

force of racket on ball

[**2** marks, **1** mark for each arrow]

b) push [**1**]

2. a)

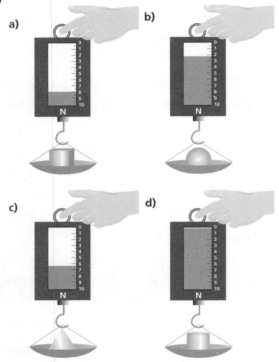

a)

b)

c)

d)

[**4**]

b) He will have to use a larger Newton meter. [**1**]

3.

Angle of ramp (°)	Distance to marker (cm)	Time taken (s)	Speed (cm/s)
10	30	2.5	12.0
20	30	**1.9**	15.7
30	30	1.2	**25**
40	30	**0.9**	33.3
50	30	0.8	37.5

[**3**]

4. a) *Points plotted, with line of best fit:*

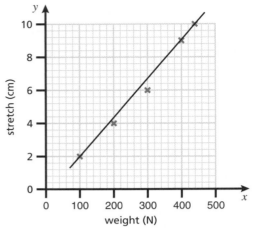

[**2** marks, **1** mark for plotting points correctly, **1** mark for line of best fit]

Graphs often appear in test papers. Make sure that you know how to draw them the correct size and always plot the points using small 'x's.

b) Hooke's Law means the stretch is directly proportional to the load applied [**1**]. The spring obeys this law because the graph shows a straight line, with approximately 2 cm of stretch for every 100 N [**1**].

Pages 174–175 Exploring Contact and Non-Contact Forces

1. N S / S N
   S / N
   S N / N S
   or
   [**1**]

2. a) The rod will repel / move away. [**1**]
   b) The rods both have the same charge, so they will repel. [**1**]
   c) The rods will be attracted to each other. [**1**]

3. a) The gerbils' feet have a very large area (they are ski shaped) [**1**]. This helps stop the gerbil from sinking in the sand as the pressure will be lower [**1**].
   b) $4 \times 2400 \text{ cm}^2 = 9600 \text{ cm}^2$ [**1**]
   4500 N / 9600 cm^2 = 0.47 N/cm^2 [**2**]

A large proportion of students lose marks because they do not show the working out to a question. It's worth the effort as you may pick up marks even if the final answer is incorrect.

4. There will be less water displaced in the Channel as there is more upthrust; fresh water contains less dissolved salts, so upthrust will be lower. **[2]**

Pages 176–177 Motion on Earth and in Space

1. 200 N **[1]**

2. **a)** B, C, D, A **[1]**

b) 16 m in 11 min

16 m / 11 min = 1.45 m/min **[1]**

or 11 min (11 x 60 s) = 660 s

16 m / 660 s = 0.024 m/s **[1]**

> A large proportion of students lose marks because they do not show the working out to a question. It's worth the effort as you may pick up marks even if the final answer is incorrect.

3. **a)** 0 m/s *or* he does not appear to be moving **[1]**

b) 120 km/h **[1]**

4. **a)** gravity **[1]**

b) They would orbit closer to the larger star. **[1]**

5. **a)** **i)** 21st March; **ii)** 21st December; **iii)** 21st September; **iv)** 21st June **[2]**

b) In the southern hemisphere during summer, day length gets progressively longer. **[1]**

6. **a)** 298 N **[1]**

b) 800 N (accept 784 N) **[1]**

Pages 178–179 Energy Transfers and Sound

1. **a)** A **[1]**

b) E **[1]**

c) 600 J **[1]**

2. **a)** cream cracker **[1]**

b) fuel / food + oxygen ➔ carbon dioxide + water + energy **[1]**

c) chemical energy **[1]** to heat **[1]** and light **[1]** energy.

3. Sound needs a medium to travel through **[1]**. A solid has particles closer together than in air **[1]**, therefore the sound energy is passed through the railway line faster **[1]**.

4. ultrasound has a frequency higher than 20,000 Hz; ultrasound does not harm the baby **[2]**

5. **a)** sound waves hit the window causing it to vibrate **[1]**

b) The sound waves would dissipate if the room were larger **[1]** and so would not have enough energy to make the window vibrate **[1]**.

Pages 180–181 Magnetism and Electricity

1. **a)** A **[1]**

b)

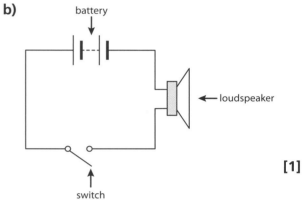

[1]

c) cell / battery **[1]**

> When drawing circuits, use a ruler for the wires and leave no gaps.

2. **a)**

Voltage (V)	Current (A)	Resistance (Ω)
2	0.5	**4**
6	**2**	3
8	2	4

[3]

b) The opposition to the flow of current through an object. **[1]**

3. **a)** increasing the number of coils increases the strength of the electromagnet. **[1]**

b) increase current / voltage; add a steel core **[2]**

c) Iron because you want to be able to turn an electromagnet on and off **[1]**. Iron loses its magnetism whereas steel does not **[1]**.

4. The Earth has a core that produces a magnetic field **[1]**, like a bar magnet. Navigation compasses follow the magnetic field lines **[1]** to point North **[1]**.

Pages 182–183 Waves and Energy Transfer

1. **a)** A = 14 Hz; B = 4 Hz; C = 4.7 Hz; D = 1.3 Hz

[4]

b)

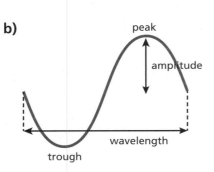

[**2** marks, **1** mark for peak and trough correctly identified, **1** mark for wavelength and amplitude correctly identified]

2. After the sound wave is recorded it is then played back so that the peak of the recorded wave matches the trough of the actual wave and vice versa **[1]**. This means that the external sound wave cancels out **[1]**.

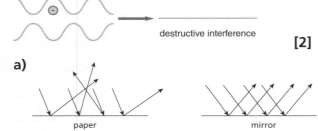

destructive interference

[2]

3. **a)**

paper   mirror

[**1** mark for paper reflections being scattered. **1** mark for mirror reflected rays being parallel. **1** mark for having incident rays all parallel.]

b)

Experiment	Angle of incidence (°)	Angle of reflection (°)
1	25	**25**
2	**60**	60
3	90	**90**

[3]

c) Experiment 3 **[1]**

4. **a)**

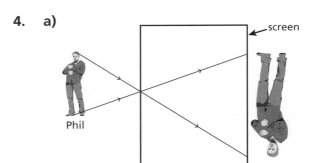

pinhole camera

[**1** mark for the rays drawn (no gaps). **1** mark for arrows in correct direction.]

b)

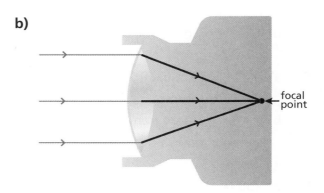

[**1** mark for the three rays correctly drawn (with no gaps). **1** mark for arrows in correct direction. **1** mark for all rays passing through labelled focal point.]

1. **a)**

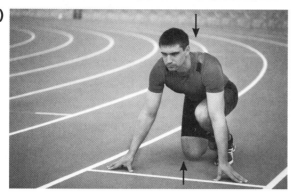

Two arrows drawn, both same size but in opposite direction. Weight down, reaction from ground up. **[2]**

b) 700 N (*accept 686 N*) **[1]**

c) speed = distance / time

= 1600 m / ((5 x 60) + 30) s

= 1600 m / 330 s

= 4.8 m/s

[**2** marks, **[1]** for working out, **[1]** for answer with correct unit]

d) speed = distance / time

rearranged to: time = distance / speed

time = 1600 m / 5.3 m/s

= 302 s *or* 5 min 2 s

[**2** marks, **[1]** for working out, **[1]** for answer with correct unit]

e) **i)** 1.8 N **[1]**

ii) Mars 0.67 N

Neptune 2.2 N **[both correct for 1]**

iii) 1750 N **[1]**

f) Mass **[1]**

2. **a)**

Plant cell	Animal cell
Cell wall	Cytoplasm
Chloroplast	Membrane
Cytoplasm	Mitochondria
Mitochondria	Nucleus
Nucleus	
Vacuole	
Membrane	

[7]

[**1** mark for correct placement of each word]

Humans are an example of an animal.

b)

Made of lots of cells	M
Cells perform many different jobs	U
Each cell depends upon many other cells	M
Cells are specialised	M
Made of just one cell	U

[5]

Learn your definitions, e.g. unicellular and multicellular.

c) tissue before organ **[1]**

organ before system **[1]**

system before organism **[1]**

d)

Body cell from mum and dad 46 46

Sperm and ova cells 23 23

Fertilised cell 46 **[5]**

Sperm and ova always contain half the number of chromosomes cells in the rest of the body.

e) Nucleus – part of the cell that contains the chromosomes.

Chromosome – a length of DNA that consists of many different genes.

Gene – a single instruction for making one protein. **[3]**

Try to make sure connecting lines are drawn using a ruler.

f) **i)** movement of molecules **[1]** from an area of high concentration **[1]** to an area of low concentration **[1]**

ii) *answers will vary but could include*: the movement of oxygen from lungs to blood; carbon dioxide from blood to lungs; or movement of glucose from cell to cell [2]

3. a) i) gnome and playhouse [2]
       ii) copper weather vane [1]
       iii) bird bath [1]
    b) iron + oxygen + water → rust [2]
       [**1** mark for correct reactants; **1** mark for correct product]
    c) coat with paint / plastic [1] because this will stop oxygen and water getting to it [1]. [*Do not accept* don't leave outside or an answer that implies removing oxygen / water from the air.]
    d) low melting point; low density; gas at room temperature. [All correct [2], two correct [1]]
    e) i) composite [1]
       ii) carbon fibre has a very high strength to weight ratio [1]; carbon fibre is very light [1]

4. a) alcohol – anaerobic; glucose – both; lactic acid – anaerobic; oxygen – both [4]
       [**1** mark for correct placement of each word]
    b) lactic acid is produced in humans but not in yeast; carbon dioxide is produced in yeast but not in humans [2]

Only use the number of ticks the question asks for.

    c) There is not always sufficient oxygen available. [1]
    d) 1 × 30 = x × 5
       x = 6 (Newtons)
       [**1** mark for correct formula. **1** mark for substituting the correct numbers. **1** mark for correct answer.]

Make sure you show your working out. You may still score 1 or 2 marks even if you get the final answer wrong.

    e) *Any 2 of*: store excess food as fat; put on weight; would become obese [2]
    f) 2500 x 4.2 = 10,500 kJ [2]
    g) no sunlight energy at night; plants use respiration to release energy in the dark [2]

5. a) A pencil-drawn line will not move up the paper along with the sample pigments. [1]
    b) The most soluble colourings travel the furthest. [1]
    c) E121 [1]
    d)
    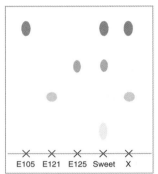
    E105 E121 E125 Sweet X [2]
    e) The sweet is not suitable as it contains E125, which is a banned dye [1].
       I reached this conclusion because there is a dot matching E125 in the sweet sample as well as the E125 sample [1].
    f) The ink in permanent marker is not water soluble *or* the ink is only soluble in alcohol. [1]

6. a) *Ray of light continues and is bent (refracted)* [1] *and refracted again when it leaves the prism* [1]. *There should be no gaps in rays.*

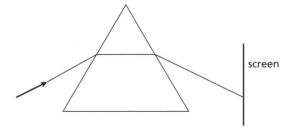
screen

b) red **[1]**

c) red, green, blue (any order) **[1]**

d) i)

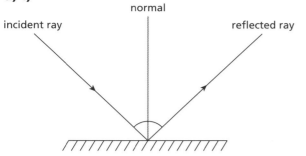

Incident ray drawn with ruler, arrow in correct direction and at 45 degrees +/− 5 degrees. **[1]** *Reflected ray drawn with ruler, arrow in correct direction and at 45 degrees +/− 5 degrees. No gaps.* **[1]**

ii) The angle of incidence equals the angle of reflection. **[1]**

e) The image is upside down because the ray of light from the top of the object enters the pinhole on the camera and moves in a straight line to the bottom of the screen **[1]**. The ray of light from the bottom moves in a straight line through the hole to the top of the screen **[1]**.

7. a) Naomi can see bubbles in the test tubes (which means a gas is being formed). **[1]**

b)

Metal	Salt
Tin	Tin sulfate
Iron	Iron sulfate
Magnesium	Magnesium sulfate

All correct for **[1]**. *Spelling of sulfate or sulphate accepted. Do not accept sulphite.*

c) copper, tin, iron, magnesium
All correct for **[1]**. *If symbols used, they must be completely correct, i.e. Cu, Sn, Fe and Mg.*

d) *Diagram needs to have more bubbles than the one with iron. To be sure of a mark draw at least eight bubbles.* **[1]**

e) Nothing would happen. This is because the iron is already chemically joined to sulfate, so it will not displace it. **[1]**

f) $Ca(s) + H_2SO_4(aq) \rightarrow CaSO_4(aq) + H_2(g)$
[1] *for left hand side of equation,* **[1]** *for right hand side,* **[1]** *for all state symbols correct.*

8. a) crop – 1; moths – 10; dormice – 100; foxes – 1000 **[4]**

The numbers always increase as you move along the food chain.

b) Plants provide animals with food.
Animals provide plants with carbon dioxide.
Plants provide animals with oxygen. **[3]**

Only use the number of ticks the question asks for.

c) large surface area – to collect as much sunlight energy as possible; small holes on the underside of the leaf – to allow carbon dioxide into the leaf and oxygen to leave the leaf; are green in colour – contain chlorophyll for photosynthesis
All correct **[2]**, two correct **[1]**

Try to make sure connecting lines are drawn using a ruler.

d) *rings around oxygen* **[1]** *and carbon dioxide* **[1]**

Make sure the ring is clearly drawn around the word of your choice.

e) Variation can be continuous or discontinuous.
Variation increases the chance of survival when an environment changes.

[2]

> Only use the number of ticks the question asks for.

f)

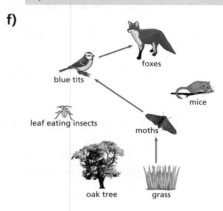

Arrow from grass to moths **[1]**;
arrow from moths to blue tits **[1]**
arrow from blue tits to foxes **[1]**

This page has been left blank

This page has been left blank

This page has been left blank

Revision Tips

Rethink Revision

Have you ever taken part in a quiz and thought '*I know this*!', but no matter how hard you scrabbled around in your brain you just couldn't come up with the answer?

It's very frustrating when this happens, but in a fun situation it doesn't really matter. However, in tests and assessments, it is essential that you can recall the relevant information when you need to.

Most students think that revision is about making sure you **know** *stuff*, but it is also about being confident that you can **retain** that *stuff* over time and **recall** it when needed.

Revision that Really Works

Experts have found that there are two techniques that help with *all* of these things and consistently produce better results in tests and exams compared to other revision techniques.

Applying these techniques to your KS3 revision will ensure you get better results in tests and assessments and will have all the relevant knowledge at your fingertips when you start studying for your GCSEs.

It really isn't rocket science either – you simply need to:
*   **test yourself** on each topic as many times as possible
*   **leave a gap** between the test sessions.

It is most effective if you leave a good period of time between the test sessions, e.g. between a week and a month. The idea is that just as you start to forget the information, you force yourself to recall it again, keeping it fresh in your mind.

Three Essential Revision Tips

1 Use Your Time Wisely
*   Allow yourself plenty of time
*   Try to start revising six months before tests and assessments – it's more effective and less stressful
*   Your revision time is precious so use it wisely – using the techniques described on this page will ensure you revise effectively and efficiently and get the best results
*   Don't waste time re-reading the same information over and over again – it's time-consuming and not effective!

2 Make a Plan
*   Identify all the topics you need to revise (this Complete Revision & Practice book will help you)
*   Plan at least five sessions for each topic
*   A one-hour session should be ample to test yourself on the key ideas for a topic
*   Spread out the practice sessions for each topic – the optimum time to leave between each session is about one month but, if this isn't possible, just make the gaps as big as realistically possible.

3 Test Yourself
*   Methods for testing yourself include: quizzes, practice questions, flashcards, past-papers, explaining a topic to someone else, etc.
*   This Complete Revision & Practice book gives you seven practice test opportunities per topic
*   Don't worry if you get an answer wrong – provided you check what the right answer is, you are more likely to get the same or similar questions right in future!

Visit our website to download your free flashcards, for more information about the benefits of these revision techniques and for further guidance on how to plan ahead and make them work for you.

www.collins.co.uk/collinsks3revision